"This book will change the way you approach writing! Martha Alderson's Scene Tracker and Plot Planner tools have helped hundreds of workshop and conference attendees hone their skills, and now you can learn how to take the fear out of plotting even if you can't attend one of her workshops. If you only buy one writing book this year, buy *Blockbuster Plots*!"
    –**Melanie Rigney**, former *Writer's Digest Magazine* editor

"Few writing teachers understand the subtleties of plot as deeply, or can explain them as clearly as Martha Alderson. Her Plot book is a great gift for aspiring storytellers. It's that rarest of writing tools -- one that will not only add life and sparkle to your plot, but also unleashes the magic that lies at the core of your story. A must have."
    –**Frank Baldwin**, author of *Balling the Jack* and *Jake & Mimi*

"Martha Alderson, the 'Plotting Queen' introduced me to the front story/back story concept while I was weaving *Love Made of Heart*. This extraordinary teacher came through again, with her book! Just in time for me to finish weaving another novel!"
    –**Teresa LeYung Ryan**, author and community member who encourages everyone to step into their dreams. **www.LoveMadeOfHeart.com**

"An exciting new approach to understanding plot from a writing expert and educational expert, the unique Scene Tracker and Plot Planner system is guaranteed to help writers master this elusive craft. Blockbuster Plots is unique in the marketplace; no other fiction writing guide offers tools like the Scene Tracker and Plot Planner."
    –**Adrinda Kelly**, acquisition editor **McGraw-Hill**

"For those stumbling in the dark forest of plotting, Alderson's book is a godsend. Clear instructions show how to use graphs and charts for identifying problems in fiction, along with examples from the novels of Rick Bragg, Janet Finch, Mark Twain, and Ernest J. Gaines."
    –**Sal Glynn**, former editor of Ten Speed Press and author of
    The Dog Walked Down the Street

"Any writer seeking to produce not just acceptable but superior works must have this guide."
   –Midwest Book Review

"Martha does a fine job of explaining the aspects of scene and plot, and the book is geared towards the anxious writer, which I feel makes it unique. The Scene Tracker and Plot Planner are effective, straightforward methods of making the elements of story that can seem amorphous, concrete. It's a good diagnostic tool. Congratulations of producing a good-looking, important book for writers."
   –Kimberley Cameron, literary agent

"My computer crashed this weekend--which allowed me to stay away from the screen and look at your book. I got out my pencil and marked stuff as I read. I just finished this morning--it's a great book. And I think it should be helpful to many people (including myself)."
   –Jana McBurney Lin, author of the award-winning novel:
   My Half of the Sky

"Even the seasoned and super-successful writer will find this chatty but superbly planned book refreshing, stimulating, and sometimes even positively corrective. The abundance of white space and the frequent reminders make for easy reading. The appendices are worth the price of the book!"
   –Barbara Smith, author of *Six Miles Out* and *The Circumstance of Death*.
   Writer's Digest Judge, self-published books, chairwoman emerita of
   Alderson-Broaddus College's Division of Humanities and a medical ethicist.

"The Scene Tracker is a great tool for writers. It helps the writer keep track of what belongs in a scene, and teaches her how to build scenes that are multi-layered. I use Martha's model with my students and to help my own writing."
   –LJ Myers, author of *Becoming Whole: Writing Your Healing Story*,
   Don't Call Me Mother, The Music Man, Who Am I, Anyway?

BLOCKBUSTER PLOTS
PURE AND SIMPLE

Take the Panic Out of Plot

Martha Alderson, M.A.

Illusion Press
Los Gatos, California

ISBN 978-1-877809-19-4

Published by Illusion Press
708 Blossom Hill Road #146
Los Gatos, CA 95032
www.illusionpress.com

Cover art by Shreve Stockton
Copyediting by Melanie Rigney

First Edition 2004

Printed on recycled paper by DeHart's Media Services

THIS WORKBOOK IS DEDICATED to my husband, Bobby Ray, for always believing.

CONTENTS

PLOT PLANNER

APPENDICES

ACKNOWLEDGMENTS

I WISH TO ACKNOWLEDGE all of the writers who volunteered to road-test the techniques offered in this book and whose feedback I found invaluable: Anna, Luisa, Claire, P. A., Jim, Jana, Kara, Clare, Sheila, Mary, Denise, Robin, Sarah, Roya and Linda Joy; Katie Burdick for providing me a glimpse of what was to be; Luisa Adams for everything I know about the body and creativity; Teresa LeYung Ryan for her heart and endless support, Julie Madsen and Beth Proudfoot for instilling in me a spirit of enthusiasm, excitement and expectancy; and Shreve Stockton for the amazing cover. I especially wish to thank all my students; the inspired editorial guidance and persistent belief of Melanie Rigney; and the gentle reassurances of Patricia Hamilton. This book came out in spite of me for the greatest possible good of writers everywhere.

INTRODUCTION

ARE YOU CONFUSED about plot? You are not alone. Plot took me years to pin down. I attended all sorts of writing workshops, but found much of the information difficult to translate to the page. I read all sorts of books on the craft of writing. The advice generally boiled down to putting your character in a pickle and seeing what happens next. This technique works for many successful writers, but it did not work for me.

I longed for something more concrete, not a formula per se, but specific guidelines to help bring depth to my story lines. I searched for anything I could find that directly addressed the issue of plot development. Unable to find much, I berated myself for not grasping what everyone else seemed to understand. I even quit writing for a spell, reasoning that if I were truly meant to be a writer, it would come more easily for me. But the muse continued to haunt me. Over time, I came to realize that everyone else was struggling with plot; they just were not talking about it.

Through years of perseverance and determination, I pinned down the elusive concept of plot to the point where I could actually "see" it. Wanting to save others the frustration I had experienced and using what I know about how people learn, I started teaching plot to writers. *BLOCKBUSTER PLOTS Pure and Simple (BBP)* came out of that passion.

In workshops and private consultations, I have witnessed what happens when writers delve more deeply into the dynamics of cause and effect. If you explore how well-constructed characters in conflict act as the driving force behind an exceptional story, you will be better able to create your own exceptional stories. Explore the themes of your own life, and your projects will have lasting meaning.

PLOT is a series of
  scenes
arranged by
  cause and effect
to create
  dramatic action
filled with
  tension and conflict
to further the
  character's
  emotional
  development
and create
  thematic significance.

TECHNIQUES
I offer in *BLOCKBUSTER PLOTS Pure and Simple* have helped hundreds of writers create dramatic action plots and heighten tension and suspense in scenes as well as in the overall project.

WRITING has its own way of creating enough self-doubt.

A CLEARLY FORMULATED PLOTLINE helps you get going, prevents you from stalling partway through, and guarantees that even those who typically never finish anything will make it to the end.

INSPIRATION (the unseen) longs to be manifested through creative energy to the physical (the seen). If the muse continues to haunt you, but you are hampered by form, this is the book for you.

DVDs available at www.blockbusterplots.com

TARGET AUDIENCE

If you are having a difficult time seeing where your story is headed; or, if ideas are rolling around in your head but you are having trouble getting started; or, if your book has been rejected time and time again, you most likely need help with plot. This is the book for you.

Whether a screenwriter, a memoirist, or a writer of children's, young adult, or adult fiction, you will benefit from a firm understanding of scene and the way to develop a plotline that combines the dramatic action, character emotional development, and thematic elements of your project.

When *BBP* calls for interactive participation, you are encouraged to use your own characters and scenes. If you have not yet started a writing project, use your imagination or a book by your favorite author.

Use *BBP* in conjunction with one of my writing workshop DVDs or on your own. Either way, the techniques will change your writing life forever. For the sake of convenience, this workbook gives independent consideration to the dramatic action, character emotional development, and thematic significance of story. But keep in mind that all aspects of a successful writing project must become integrated to create unity, and achieving this unity is the goal of every writer.

CHALLENGE
How to Use this book

BLOCKBUSTER PLOTS Pure and Simple is divided into two parts: Scene Tracker and Plot Planner. Both parts are intended as a step-by-step interactive guide for maximizing your scenes and providing depth to your stories. Throughout *BBP*, you are invited to apply the techniques to your own work or, if you have not yet created something, to use the work of a writer you admire. I encourage you to use your own work, no matter how wretched you are convinced it is. Either way, all you really need to proceed is:

- A willing heart
- A copy of your manuscript or a book that you do not mind marking up
- A 6-foot strip of banner paper
- A set of markers
- A pad of Post-it notes

SCENE TRACKER

PLOT PLANNER

YOUR ABILITY TO PLOT is strengthened by doing it.

GENERALLY SPEAKING, we do not outgrow our own unique learning style. Rather, we learn to compensate.

If your heart is willing but your mind recoils from the sort of methodical, organized approach to the creative process presented in this book, I encourage you to step out of your comfort zone. One resistant writer kept moaning that she was not an organized person and that these techniques would not work for her. Yet she knew her story needed help. So, she stuck with it. Now, she encourages other resistant writers not to shut out something that might be valuable, but to confront their fears and grow as writers.

If you like to work things out on the page, so be it. But at the same time, try scanning the ideas in this book. A key element in the nature of creativity is giving yourself time to work things out. When you face your first rewrite, perhaps then you will be ready to give the techniques a try.

SENSORY FEEDBACK

In my life before writing, I founded a speech, language, and learning disability clinic for children and young adults. For more than twenty years, I interacted with thousands of children and came to appreciate firsthand the many different ways people learn.

In appreciation for all the different styles of learning, *BBP* is formatted to provide you with as much sensory feedback as possible for full discovery and for ease in learning. The more you actively participate in the process and the less passive you are, the more you will grasp. The idea is to shake things up. Do things differently and watch your piece rush at you in a completely new way.

This book is divided between explanation and activity

forms. The pencil icon in the sidebar notifies you of each "hands-on" step toward creating your own scene tracker and plot planner. The text provides straightforward explanations that will appeal to your cognition. For those of you who experience words in books as sliding off the page, each page of this book is framed. Text that is framed leads to fixed, clear images and stimulates your sense of vision. The forms throughout the book are designed to help make visible that which is invisible. Each time you fill in a form or use a marker, your sense of touch is stimulated and gives you kinesthetic feedback.

The one sense I cannot provide on these pages is the sense of hearing. If, at any point in the book, you lose your energy or passion for further exploration into your writing or if you are confronted with something that feels uncomfortably challenging, read the passages aloud. You may find that you benefit from the auditory feedback.

As a result of all my years of teaching, I have found that it is easier to welcome new material when we stay open and loose. Therefore, I would like to suggest you breathe and stay relaxed. We have all been taught to try harder when we come up against a challenge. But actually, the harder we try, the tenser we become, closing off our ability to absorb and assimilate new information. The picture of a tea cup in the sidebar is a reminder to stop every so often and reflect.

EXAMPLES

Throughout both parts of *BBP*, you are provided with examples of how other writers successfully accomplished the tasks offered. The examples are intended to empower you.

Many of the examples are from Pulitzer Prize-winning

TRY SURRENDERING to the possibilities, and you very well might find yourself enjoying the experience.

THIS BOOK
offers guidelines, not rules.

fiction. Let me assure you that I did not choose these brilliant examples of scene and plot to intimidate you. Rather, I use them with the firm belief that the stories came to their authors just as your story will come to you: through a lot of hard work and many rewrites.

The exploration into scene and plot will ensure that with each new rewrite you will give your story a sharper focus and greater depth.

WHAT TO EXPECT

If you are an intuitive writer who likes to find your way on the page, you may find yourself overwhelmed or balking at some of the techniques offered in *BBP*. Go ahead and experience the resistance. Then find a way to make the system work for you. The ideas presented here are left-brained sorts of activities. You likely feel more comfortable on the other side. However, these techniques will support your intuitive side in defining the boundaries in which to create. This process will ultimately help your writing. What I offer here can and should be revised in any way that serves your writing.

Signs are posted along the way to help facilitate learning. For example, there is a stop sign at the end of Chapter 3. For those of you who benefit from immediate, experiential, hands-on learning, this is a spot where you put this book down and pick up your own project. If you choose to stop at the stop signs, go ahead and try out the technique and organization until you are ready to move on.

If at any point while you are working on the techniques offered in *BBP* you feel inspired to go back to the actual writing of your story, by all means put this book down and do so.

Remember, the ideas offered in *BBP* are not rules. They are simply loose guidelines that are intended to be bent, ignored, and adapted in whatever way best supports your storytelling.

SCENE TRACKER

A good scene advances the plot of the story, develops the character, contributes to the theme, provides tension and conflict, and/or reflects a change in attitude or circumstances. A great scene does all of these at once. The Scene Tracker is a form that helps you see all of the important layers of each of your scenes side-by-side and step-by-step from the beginning to the end of your project.

PLOT PLANNER

Once you have your scenes in order, it is time to plan your plot. Plot springs from character in conflict. Not only will you learn about action, character, and thematic plot, you have the opportunity to practice using the scenes on your Scene Tracker to create a plotline for your latest project.

AT THE VERY HEART of this book is the intention to help keep you at the task of writing.

TO PURCHASE a copy of the Scene Tracker Template CD or the Scene Tracker Writers Workshop DVD, please go to www.blockbusterplots.com

TO PURCHASE a copy of the Plot Planner Writers Workshop DVD, please visit: www.blockbusterplots.com

SCENE TRACKER

INTRODUCTION

At its best, each and every single scene advances the dramatic action plot, develops the character, contributes to the theme, provides tension and conflict, and reflects a change in attitude or circumstances.

In my plot-intensive workshops, it quickly becomes apparent that many writers are as confused about scene as they are about plot. Many writers think they are writing a scene when in fact they are writing a summary. Their scenes have no real beginning, middle, or end—the basic core structure of scene that mimics an overall plot. Due to confusion, most writers are not making the most of scene for the greater good of the story.

SCENE TRACKER

Whether a screenwriter, a memoirist, or a writer of children's, young adult, or adult fiction, you write countless scenes. How does one make the most of all these scenes and keep track of all the information? A simple technique is to create a visual representation of your story called a Scene Tracker. In creating a Scene Tracker for your project, you discover exactly where your strengths and weaknesses lie. The Scene Tracker also works especially well for sorting out all the threads of your project, saving you both time and effort.

The Scene Tracker tracks scene by scene all the dates and settings; the character's emotional development and goals; the dramatic action; conflict; and the thematic significance, so that the whole does not become a tangled mess. Think of the Scene Tracker as the loom that holds your story ideas, scene

SCENE is at the core structure of story.

SCENES MAKE PLOT. When I became determined to unravel the mysteries of plot, I knew I needed to back up and get pure and simple.

THE SCENE TRACKER helps you interweave all the threads for a successful narrative.

BUILD YOUR SCENE TRACKER on:
- banner paper
- 11 X 17 sheets of paper
- a white board
- your computer

MY HOPE FOR YOU is that your search for the truth through your writing remains active and honored.
We each share the need to be heard.
We each have something vital to offer.

fragments, character development, snippets of dialogue, research and details, tension and conflict in roughly the order you envision the story will unfold. When you start out, you may have lots of holes and gaps in your Scene Tracker. These will be filled in as you come to know your story and characters better.

LAYOUT

I like to build my Scene Trackers on pieces of banner paper so I can hang them on the wall beside my computer screen. This way, my scene information is fully visible at all times. When inspiration strikes, I slap a Post-it note on the Scene Tracker rather than filing it in a folder hidden away in a file cabinet.

If you do not have the space to hang something as large as a piece of banner paper or are just not inclined to have slabs of banner paper wallpapering your rooms, try something smaller. If you travel a great deal and want your story information readily available to you, consider purchasing a Scene Tracker Template CD at www.blockbusterplots.com.

The computer method would not be as effective for me as a big piece of banner paper on the wall because the scene information would not be visible enough. But what counts is what works best for you. Just make sure that you print out your Scene Tracker and create some sort of system so that it is as visible and readily available as possible.

If you have already written a draft or two, the Scene Tracker will help with your rewrites. Use it to determine whether scenes and transitions, characters' emotional changes, and your use of detail are contributing to the fullest in the project's development.

This process may appear daunting or tedious to you. If so, at least try tracking several scenes at the beginning of your project so that you get a sense of your strengths and weaknesses in developing scene. Then, once you have tried out the system and have developed an understanding of what is important, track by chapters rather than by scenes.

Or, track only the sections of your story that appear weak to you so that you gain a better understanding of what might be missing. Or, simply track the scenes that lead up to the important turning points of your project, say the crisis and/or the climax of your book. Keep in mind that this is a system intended to help you with your writing. Find a method that works best for you and use it.

As one writer declared: "Using the Scene Tracker is like learning a new language or entering an alien culture. Many writers just think that they need to let the muse move them in any direction. Using the Scene Tracker, for me, involved adopting a new perspective on what I have written and that was an anxiety-producing proposition." This same writer persevered. Like her, as long as you take a deep breath and continue, your writing life will never be the same.

Each element of the Scene Tracker is given independent consideration. The examples provided show how successful writers integrated each of these aspects into a total structure to achieve unity.

There are no rules when it comes to writing fiction. Every idea I present to you can be approached in another way. Every Pulitzer Prize winner who followed mainstream advice can be matched by one who broke all the rules. Still, although no one way works for every writer, the ideas of scene and plot I put forward in *BLOCKBUSTER PLOTS Pure and Simple* have helped hundreds of other writers.

The deepest quality of a work of art will always be the quality of the mind of the producer...No good novel will ever proceed from a superficial mind.
—Henry James

UNDERSTAND SCENE
and you begin to understand
the essence of plot.

F O R M A T

Chapters 1-3 explain how to create a Scene Tracker. Chapters 4-11 offer specific examples from published works for each step in the development of a Scene Tracker.

Throughout the *BLOCKBUSTER PLOTS Pure and Simple*, the following definition of plot is used. For now, do not worry about what the definition means. I just want you to notice the significance of scene in the overall definition of plot.

PLOT is a series of <u>SCENES</u>
arranged by cause and effect
to create dramatic action filled with
tension and conflict to further the characters'
emotional development and provide
thematic significance.

I know; this is the most complicated definition you have ever read. Plot will become clearer to you in the second part of this book, Plot Planner, but for now, I want you to see the importance of scene in the development of plot.

Scene slows down the story speed and is written moment-by-moment for maximum effect. Scene is focused motion with tension and conflict. Not all scenes have really big events. But every scene has layers and layers of information packed into the moment. If you can convince readers to trust you with the small things up front, they will believe you with the big things to come.

SCENE
IDENTIFICATION

GETTING STARTED

Take out the piece of writing you have chosen to work with, preferably your own. Next, close your eyes and take a couple of deep breaths. Relax. Concentrate on your breathing. There is no right or wrong in what I am offering here. These are ideas that have helped other writers. I offer them to you so that you do not have to go it alone.

Now, go through the piece of writing you are working on and, page by page, mark each section where you believe a scene begins and where it ends. (Marking pens work great.)

Confused about what is a scene and what is summary? Refer to Chapter 2 for explanations and examples of Scene and Summary. If you are confident about your ability to identify scene versus summary, bypass Chapter 2 altogether and move directly to Chapter 3.

SCENE:
- Shows outward action.
- Scene is in the now, the physical, moment by moment.
- Dialogue is a scene marker.
- Action is too.

EXERCISE:
Page by page, mark where each scene begins and ends until you tire of the activity.

For more tips on Scene, go to www.blockbusterplots.com and click on Plot Tips.

If you enjoy multitasking, use a different colored marker to mark the summaries at the same time you identify scenes. Do not make a list of the scenes and summaries. Mark directly on your manuscript.

TAKE A BREAK

Get up and make yourself a cup of tea. Now, sit back and look over your manuscript. Is there a pattern made visible in the markings? Take a deep breath. Invite in the spirit of discovery. See your story in your mind.

SCENE VERSUS SUMMARY

SCENE

Charlie felt the hot rush of shot fly past his face,
and his legs shook under him with the boom of
the gun. But it was a clean miss, and he started
to run at Jerry, closing the distance even as
Jerry fished in his pocket for another load.
Twenty feet …
Jerry cursed and broke open the breech.
Twelve feet …
He slapped in the fresh shell.
Eight feet …
He snapped the gun closed.
Six feet …
He threw it to his shoulder.
Four feet …
He saw a fist the size of a lard bucket come
flying at his nose.

When you gain an appreciation for the core structure of a scene, you are able to exploit the scenes for the greater good of the story. There is another added plus: *understand scene, and plot will follow.*

A scene is written in moment by moment detail.

BE CAREFUL. Once you show in scene, do not then tell in summary to underline a point. Trust your showing abilities and trust your readers.

This is a scene from *Ava's Man* by Rick Bragg. The confrontation is a moment of most intense importance to the memoir and is being played out moment-by-moment on the page. The action in the scene is exciting. The reader's eyes speed across the page as every single step is broken down. Time slows, allowing the reader to slip into the scene. The reader feels every breath, hears the ticking of time and cringes. Which will come first, the gunshot or the fist? Tension. Conflict. This is page-turning excitement told in slow motion, told in scene.

Charlie's family may have come out on the porch to see what all the commotion was about, or there might have been traffic on the road behind them, but all that matters to this scene is what happens between these two men. In this scene, because it is so well written, no dialogue is necessary.

You will usually write many, many scenes that end up in the recycling bin. This does not mean that the scenes were not important to write. Often it is in the process of writing a scene that we, as writers, find out important information about our characters. But that does not always mean that the reader needs to read those parts. A good writer knows which scenes to keep and which scenes to cut.

The Scene Tracker will help you determine which is which.

SCENE VERSUS SUMMARY

You have likely heard the writer's mantra of: "Show, don't tell."

A scene *shows*. Summary *tells*.

Each scene has a tiny plot structure of its own, beginning with steps toward a goal or desire, followed by some sort of conflict and tension, and ending with failure or an unanswered question, or a cliffhanger, something that entices the reader to continue reading.

All conflict, confrontations, and turning points—all the high points of your story—must be played out in scene on the page, moment-by-moment in real time.

Scene is core to story, and this is where we will spend most of our time. But, since plot covers a specified period of time, from one moment to the centuries past and those to come, summary deserves at least a mention.

SUMMARY

Story is conflict shown in scene. Yet a story made up entirely of scenes can inject too much conflict and become exhausting for the reader. A summary is a place to rest. Instead of every single moment played out on the page in scene, time is compressed with summary.

Summary narrates quickly those events that are not important enough to the overall story line to *show* in detail. Summary relates those events in their sequence but compresses them or *tells* how things were during a particular period of time. The use of summary is helpful in moving quickly, so that you, as the writer, can focus on creating scenes to *show* the moments that are the most important to your plot.

> In one of my workshops, Carla, a historical fiction writer, expressed concern that her story was too long. Using the Scene Tracker, she immediately spotted the problem. She had told her story entirely in scene. Historical fiction is generally longer and broader in scope than most contemporary fiction, and so the use of summary becomes critical.

To write simply is as difficult as to be good.
—W. Somerset Maugham

CIRCUMSTANTIAL SUMMARY
sums up the circumstances of the characters over a set period of story time.

SEQUENTIAL SUMMARY
sums up the sequence of events for the characters over a set period of story time.

TWO TYPES OF SUMMARY
Circumstantial Summary

> The days went by. The women and children moved eastward through rain and bitter cold that caused their clothes and blankets to freeze during the night. So difficult was the terrain, on some days they were able to progress less than three miles.

This is an example of circumstantial summary from *True Women* by Janet Woods Windle. The passage describes the general circumstances for these women and children—what these women's lives were like on the trail and the sorts of hardships that happened to them. Because summary is telling, it sets us apart from the action. However, in this case, the author works around that by using sensory details to infuse the summary with life and immediacy.

Sequential Summary

> Consider the case of the female black leopard that escaped from the Zurich zoo in the winter of 1933. She was new to the zoo and seemed to get along with the male leopard. But various paw injuries hinted at matrimonial strife. Before any decision could be taken about what to do, she squeezed through a break in the roof bars of her cage and vanished in the night. The discovery that a wild carnivore was free in their midst created an uproar among the citizens of Zurich. Traps were set and hunting dogs were let loose.

They only rid the canton of its few half-wild dogs.
Not a trace of the leopard was found for ten
weeks. Finally, a casual labourer came upon it
under a barn twenty-five miles away and shot it.

This passage from *Life of Pi* by Yann Martel relates in sequence the events that happened over a ten-week period, but compresses them. This is an example of Sequential Summary.

If you find yourself quickly summarizing events, stop and ask: am I shying away from creating this scene because the material seems too hard, too long, or too painful to write? If the answer is yes, take a deep breath and write the events out moment by bloody moment. You may find yourself crying, sweating and swearing at the screen in front of you. Do not give up. Keep at it. Dig deep. Use the emotion.

Again, summary is important, but it is an explanation or *telling*, Scene is experiential. The more scenes you use, the more *showing* and *less telling*. The key is to find a balance. The Scene Tracker helps you do that.

USE SUMMARY TO:
- Provide information
- Fill in a character's back story
- Set up the next action
- Tell the general circumstances
- Show motive
- Change the pace
- Create a transition
- Move quickly through time

CREATING THE FORM

SEVEN FUNCTIONS OF SCENE

The technique of slowing things down forces the stakes in a story ever higher. At the same time, the stakes also rise for you the writer. Many beginning writers hide from the pressure of creating scenes by relying on summary and narration. These same writers hold the mistaken belief that *telling* what happens is a more controllable arena than *showing* in scene.

My contention is that if you break down scene to its smallest parts, you retain control.

Like plot, scene has many different layers or functions. Part One Scene Tracker of this book addresses seven of those functions for scene. There are plenty of other functions you will come up with on your own—minor character development, the villain's development, political undertones, environmental overtones, and the like. As long as you really *see* each of the seven functions discussed and developed in the Scene Tracker portion of this book, you will be better equipped to develop not only those seven, but also others in each and every scene.

Scene stretches time.

The more you understand each of the seven functions of scene, the more you will be able to deepen the meaning of your piece through nuance in subsequent rewrites.
The more you can do that, the greater your promise.

Note: Please refer to Appendix 3 for an example of how these scenes plot out on a plot planner.

EXAMPLE

Using the first three chapters from *The Adventures of Tom Sawyer* by Mark Twain, the following is an example of a Scene Tracker. The theme of this story is: there is a collective tendency of man to go overboard toward generosity and forgiveness.

For now, I just want you to have a sense of what a Scene Tracker looks like. We will go over this form step-by-step in each of the following chapters.

SCENE TRACKER — *The Adventures of Tom Sawyer* by Mark Twain

SC SU	DATES SETTING	CHARACTER EM. DEV.	GOAL	DRAMATIC ACTION	CONFLICT	CHANGE	THEME DETAIL
Chpt.1 SC #1	Fri. Aunt's House	T: Small, smart, fast, liar A:Softy Dead sis's son	Escape	Tom/Aunt Trouble	X	-/-/+	*T
SU							
SC#2	Fri. dinner		Not to be found out/cut school	Interrogated	X (Will he or won't he)	+/-/+/-	*T
SU				WHISTLING			
SC#3	Fri. Evening	Not one to fight right off	Figure out new boy	Fight Caught by A.	X (Will he or won't he)	+/-/-	Aunt forgave him earlier. Will he forgive new boy?
CHAPT.2							
SC#4	Sat. am Field	Hates work Into: J;	To get out of work	White-wash fence	X (Will he or won't he)	-/-	
SU				PAINTING			
SC#5	Minutes later	Clever	Get someone else to do work	Ignores friend Friend falls for it	X (Will he or won't he)	+/+	T. ends up with friends paying him to work

CREATE A SCENE TRACKER

To create a Scene Tracker, start by dividing a piece of paper into eight columns. I prefer to use a piece of banner paper that is about six feet long, but you can use whatever suits your individual needs.

Think of this form as the warp or foundation of your story. The first column is where you indicate what chapter you are tracking, which scene you are working on, and, when appropriate, where you indicate your summaries.

Each of the other seven columns of your Scene Tracker is for the seven functions of scene. To keep the notations in each column of the Scene Tracker separate and distinct, choose a specific color of pen or pencil for each.

SEVEN COLUMN HEADERS

Column 1 is: SCENE/SUMMARY.
This column represents the frame of your story. It is where you indicate what chapter you are tracking, which scene you are working on, and, when appropriate, where you indicate your summaries.

Column 2 is: DATES/SETTING.
This is where you plot the passage of time your story travels and, when appropriate, historical dates and events that take place during that time frame. This is also where you will indicate the setting, where the scene takes place.

Column 3 is: CHARACTER EMOTIONAL DEVELOPMENT.
Character represents the heart of your story.

Column 4 is: GOAL.
The protagonist has a specific goal in every scene that he or she hopes to attain.

TO PURCHASE a copy of the Scene Tracker template CD, go to www.blockbusterplots.com

THE SEVEN FUNCTIONS OF SCENE ARE:

- Date/Setting
- Character Emotional Development
- Goal
- Dramatic Action
- Conflict
- Change
- Thematic Details

Choose a different colored pen for each character.

BANNER PAPER is available at teacher supply stores and office supply stores.

Column 5 is: DRAMATIC/ACTION PLOT.
This column represents the front story.

Column 6 is: CONFLICT.
Story is conflict shown in scene.

Column 7 is: CHANGE.
Story is change. This is where you track the emotional changes the character moves through within each scene.

Finally, Column 8 is: THEMATIC DETAILS.
The theme is the why, the spirit of your story, your reason for writing the story, what you want your readers to take away from having read it. This column represents the border of your tapestry.

TAKE A BREAK

Before we move to the next step of filling in the Scene Tracker, sit back and really look at the form of the Scene Tracker on the banner paper. View the Scene Tracker as a visual aid in seeing the structure of your story and as a reminder that a story awaits you. Imagine where you will hang it.

When the Scene Tracker is filled in, you will see your story in ways that are not possible in simply reading what you have written. Minus the luster of words and phrases is the form of your expression. Just as it is difficult to see the forest for the trees, it is difficult to see the form of your story for the words. Mysteries and depth are hiding in your stories, right now. It is on the Scene Tracker in the interlocking plotlines that they reveal themselves.

To benefit from further straightforward explanation and specific examples of how other writers accomplish the layering of their scenes, forge on ahead to the next chapter of the workbook.

The examples I use are the first paragraph or so of the first scene from prize-winning fiction to show a variety of opening passages as well as to demonstrate and clarify the Scene Tracker organizational system.

This stop sign is posted to facilitate learning

TAKE A DEEP BREATH. See your story in your mind. Invite in the characters and the action and the spirit of discovery.

If you are the type of learner who benefits more from immediate, experiential, hands-on learning, stop here, put this book down and pick up your own manuscript.

Try the organizational system for a while, filling in what comes to you. I recommend that you use different colored markers for each column or different colored Post-it notes for your information. By using the Post-it notes, your ideas and scene development remain fluid.

If, at that point, you are inspired to write, do so. At the heart of *BLOCKBUSTER PLOTS Pure and Simple* is the intention to motivate your writing.

Do not do more than just a couple of chapters' worth of scenes. Stop when you run out of inspiration.

Hang your Scene Tracker vertically on the wall beside your computer screen, so the strip of banner paper is fully visible at all times. When inspiration strikes, slap a note on the Tracker. Never again will you lose a note in a stack of paper or file it in a folder hidden away in a file cabinet.

When you are ready, and only when you are ready, move on in this book. Chapters 4-10 provide straightforward explanations and examples of how other writers brilliantly accomplished the layering of their scenes.

START TRACKING FLASHBACKS

COLUMN 1: SCENE/SUMMARY

National Book Award winner Cormac McCarthy's *All the Pretty Horses* begins thus:

> The candleflame and the image of the candle-
> flame caught in the pierglass twisted and righted
> when he entered the hall and again when he
> shut the door. He took off his hat and came
> slowly forward. The floorboards creaked under
> his boots. In his black suit he stood in the dark
> glass where the lilies leaned so palely from their
> waisted cutglass vase. Along the cold hallway
> behind him hung the portraits of forebears only
> dimly known to him all framed in glass and dimly
> lit above the narrow wainscoting. He looked
> down at the guttered candlestub. He pressed his
> thumbprint in the warm wax pooled on the oak

veneer. Lastly he looked at the face so caved and drawn among the fold of funeral cloth, the yellowed moustache, the eyelids paper thin. That was not sleeping. That was not sleeping.

It was dark outside and cold and no wind. In the distance a calf bawled. He stood with his hat in his hand. You never combed your hair that way in your life, he said.

ANALYSIS

Scene 1 from the book's first chapter continues for another page or so. We know it is a scene because the action is being played out moment by moment. The candleflame twists. He opens and closes the door and takes off his hat. The floorboards creak. These are all the makings of scene: immediate, physical, action.

Using this example, I mark under column one on the Scene Tracker: Chpt. 1 for Chapter 1 and SC #1 for Scene 1.

SCENE TRACKER — *All the Pretty Horses* by Cormac McCarthy

SC SU	DATES SETTING	CHARACTER EM. DEV.	GOAL	DRAMATIC ACTION	CONFLICT	CHANGE	THEME DETAIL
Chpt.1 SC #1							

START TRACKING

With your Scene Tracker in front of you, refer back to your manuscript. How did you mark the beginning passage of your story with your marker? As a scene or as a summary?

Whatever your answer, indicate under Column

1/Chapter 1 and mark how your story begins: SC for scene or SU for summary.

Do not worry if you have correctly determined which it is, about being right or wrong. As you work your way through your manuscript, you will be better able to determine which is which. For now, all that really matters is that you have a passage to analyze.

If the first passage is a summary, mark SU under Column 1. Move to the next passage. Continue this way until you find your first scene. Mark that on your Scene Tracker. This is the passage you will analyze.

If you are writing a historical novel, because it is generally longer and broader in scope than most contemporary fiction, the use of summary becomes critical. Summary covers a relatively long period of time in a relatively short number of words.

This stop sign is posted to facilitate learning.
If you would rather move on with the task of
filling in your Scene Tracker, move to
Chapter 5 now.
If you have questions about flashbacks, read on.

FLASHBACKS
Linear Versus Nonlinear

At this point, invariably someone asks about flashbacks.

Seven or eight years ago, an agent told me that in her opinion, readers were no longer interested in stories told in chronological order. She believed that readers wanted to be less

RELAX
BREATHE
TRUST THE PROCESS

REMINDER:
- A scene shows outward action.
- Scene is in the now, the physical, moment by moment.
- Dialogue is a scene marker.
- Action is too.

If you choose to write in a linear fashion, starting at the very beginning, you will seldom use flashbacks. However, if you want to try for a more nonlinear approach, or just do not want to start the story at the beginning, mastery of the effective use of flashbacks becomes critical.

passive and more interactive in the story, meaning they were more interested in a nonlinear format. She might have come to this conclusion based on some of the popular fiction coming out at the time. For example, more than ten years ago, Michael Ondaatje structured *The English Patient* in a nonlinear format; his story moves forward and backward and through more than one character at a time. A few years later, David Guterson formatted *Snow Falling on Cedars* by switching effortlessly from front story to back story throughout the novel.

Since that introduction to the nonlinear format, I have seen preferences revert back to the chronological, linear story lines. For instance, Ursula Hegi begins *Stones From the River* with the protagonist's birth and tells everything that happens to the heroine, her village, and her country in sequence. Hegi uses no flashbacks because everything unfolds on the page as it happens in real story time.

Anita Diamant formats *The Red Tent* in essentially the same way except that the author starts with the mother's story and then, when her daughter is born, tells her story in chronological order with no scenes taking place before this main action of the story.

Story information is generally divided into two parts: The front story is all the events that happen in scene on the page as the story moves forward. The back story is all the history that makes the protagonist who he or she is today and why he or she sees the world in a particular way. The back story is all the history of the circumstances that are unfolding on the page. The back story helps the reader understand things in context.

Why do I say that the use of flashbacks is much abused? Sadly, we too often confuse the information that is critical for the writer to know chronologically with what is necessary to include in the text. When in doubt, writers too often revert to "telling" the back story through the use of flashbacks.

Flashback is not the only way to get in the back story information. The more difficult path is in *showing* the back story through the characters' actions and reactions, by their decision-making process and the consequences. It is worth the effort to search for just the right details your character might notice or the few, well-chosen words he or she might use in the front story as a consequence of the back story without having to resort to a flashback.

The careless use of flashbacks is one of the surest ways to break your reader from the trance. The last thing writers want to do is jar the reader from the dream they have so carefully crafted. Keeping that in mind, there are times when the effective use of a flashback or two will add significantly to the overall meaning of your story.

Flashbacks can be as short as one sentence, or they can be the longest part of the story. The one-liners can be incorporated through dialogue and description without too much fear of breaking the forward movement. Flashbacks that make up most of the story will essentially become, when well plotted, the forward-moving story line. It is the use of intermediate flashbacks that is the trickiest.

A good rule of thumb: only use flashbacks that themselves are above the line on your plotline (this will make more sense when you read Part Two Plot Planner) or are important turning points in the character's development.

When you do use flashbacks, craft them in such a way that they are full of conflict, tension, and/or suspense. This is the best way to ensure that your flashbacks deliver only the essential information that informs the present action of the story and that pushes the story forward. A well-placed and well-crafted flashback can give the reader an important context to the main character's overall development.

A flashback is a simple, though much abused, way to incorporate the back story into the front story.

I write as straight as I can, just as I walk as straight as I can, because that is the best way to get there.
—H. G. Wells

GUIDELINES FOR THE USE OF FLASHBACKS

Once you are convinced that a flashback is critical to the story, here are some ways to use flashbacks effectively:

1) Do not use too many of them—less is more.

2) Plot out your flashbacks and give them their own conflict and tension (a mini-story within the story).

3) Bring in the past only when it has a direct bearing on what is happening in the present.

4) Start the story by firmly grounding the readers in the who, what, when, where, and why of the front story before going into a flashback. First, hook the reader. Tell the reader what is at stake in the front story, and then flash to the past.

5) Before you go into the back story, leave the reader with a memorable and authentic detail at a high or low place in the story. When you return to present time, use that detail again. This way, readers will recognize when they are leaving the front story for the back story and when they are returning.

6) If you are writing your front story in present tense, then the flashback will be in simple past tense. (For example: Times were not always this miserable. When we were small, we used to laugh until we cried.) If past tense is used for the primary action or the front story, then shift into past perfect, using the word "had" for the flashback. (For example: Times had not always been this miserable. When we had been small, we had laughed until we cried.) "Had" will alert the reader that the past is being introduced. If the flashback is long, use "had" once or twice to establish the time frame and continue with the simple past.

7) Use space breaks on either side of a flashback.

8) Come right out and mention the date or time going into the flashback and then again coming out of the flashback.

When in doubt, be clever.

For those of you who have written a draft or two of your project and have employed the use of flashback, take some time now to read over your work. The development of a flashback can be a time for you as the writer to get to know your characters better, a chance to delve deeper into their essence or their history. Once you know that information, you likely have incorporated it in less intrusive ways. Yes? Then cut the flashback. No? See if you can come up with ways to incorporate the information into the front story without having to resort to the use of a flashback. Either way, if you no longer need the flashback, cut it.

If at any time during the tracking of your story, you do come across a flashback, indicate that under the Scene/Summary heading. This way, you can track how many flashbacks you have and where they occur.

EXAMPLE:

If your story begins in flashback and the flashback is written in scene, then mark Column 1 thus:

SCENE TRACKER

SC SU	DATES SETTING	CHARACTER EM. DEV.	GOAL	DRAMATIC ACTION	CONFLICT	CHANGE	THEME DETAIL
Chpt.1 FLB/ SC #1							

DATE
SETTING
RESEARCH

COLUMN 2: DATES/SETTING

The classic *The Sea-Wolf* by Jack London opens in circumstantial summary:

> I scarcely know where to begin, though I sometimes facetiously place the cause of it all to Charley Furuseth's credit. He kept a summer cottage in Mill Valley, under the shadow of Mount Tamalpais, and never occupied it except when he loafed through the winter months and read Nietzsche and Schopenhauer to rest his brain. When summer came on, he elected to sweat out a hot and dusty existence in the city and to toil incessantly. Had it not been my custom to run up to see him every Saturday afternoon and to stop

over till Monday morning, this particular January Monday morning would not have found me afloat on San Francisco Bay.

ANALYSIS

RELAX.
It never comes from pushing.

Many works that are considered more literary than genre begin with a description in summary of the story's ordinary world to give the reader a feel of the time. We know *Sea-Wolf* begins in summary, because in the passage he is not taking us through the action moment by moment. He is telling us, or describing, the general circumstances during this period: how things were, the sorts of things that usually or frequently happened and what got him into his current situation.

Therefore, on the Scene Tracker we mark in Column 1 SU for Summary. Although we also learn that it is January on a Monday morning, we do not put that on the Scene Tracker at this point because we do not track information in summaries on the Scene Tracker. We only track the scenes.

SCENE TRACKER — *The Sea-Wolf* by Jack London

SC SU	DATES SETTING	CHARACTER EM. DEV.	GOAL	DRAMATIC ACTION	CONFLICT	CHANGE	THEME DETAIL
Chpt.1 SU							

However, London begins the fourth paragraph of Chapter 1 thus:

A red-faced man, slamming the cabin door behind him and stumping out on the deck, interrupted my reflections, though I made a mental note of the topic for use in a projected essay which I had thought of calling "The Necessity for

Freedom: A plea for the Artist." The red-faced man shot a glance up at the pilothouse, gazed around at the fog, stumped across the deck and back (he evidently had artificial legs), and stood still by my side, legs wide apart, and with an expression of keen enjoyment on his face. I was not wrong when I decided that his days had been spent on the sea.

Now we can begin tracking because we have the beginning of an actual scene. Scene 1 from Chapter 1 continues for almost seven pages. We know it is a scene because the action is being played out moment by moment.

SCENE TRACKER — *The Sea-Wolf* by Jack London

SC SU	DATES SETTING	CHARACTER EM. DEV.	GOAL	DRAMATIC ACTION	CONFLICT	CHANGE	THEME DETAIL
Chpt.1 SU							
SC#1	Jan. Mon. a.m.						

PREVIOUS EXAMPLE

1) To continue the example from Chapter 4, in the paragraph following the opening passage, McCarthy writes in *All the Pretty Horses:* "… a thin gray reef beginning along the eastern rim of the world," and thus all we know about the timing is that the scene takes place just before dawn.

SCENE TRACKER — *All the Pretty Horses* by Cormac McCarthy

SC SU	DATES SETTING	CHARACTER EM. DEV.	GOAL	DRAMATIC ACTION	CONFLICT	CHANGE	THEME DETAIL
Chpt.1 SC#1	Just before dawn						

**RELAX
BREATHE
TRUST THE PROCESS**

Instead of waiting for inspiration to hit, show up to write and to plot at the same time every day. Inspiration will follow.

CONTINUE TRACKING

With your Scene Tracker in front of you, refer back to your manuscript. Fill in Column 2 with when your story begins— the season, year, and/or time of day. Include any real-life historical events and political issues that occur during this time.

If you chose a different color of pen for each column heading of the Scene Tracker to keep the information separate and distinct, keep the same color for your notations in each column.

EXPLANATION

Even if your story does not directly involve true historical events, one way to add more depth to your story is by including at least one major and one minor historical event, as well as a trivial event. This will provide you with a perspective of what is happening in the setting, country, and world during the time period in which you are writing. Historical events, especially the big ones, can provide useful information with which to thicken the plot.

For example, the historical novel I am currently writing begins in February 1968, a time of cataclysmic upheaval, a time in history when the great divide of class and culture no longer kept people separated, however different they might be. For the purpose of my Scene Tracker, I abbreviate that to "Great Divide" and add it under the date. Following that is a more specific historical event: the first United Farm Workers Benefit held at Fillmore West in San Francisco featuring the band Santana or, my abbreviation, "UFW."

SCENE TRACKER — *Parallel Lives* by Martha Alderson

SC SU	DATES SETTING	CHARACTER EM. DEV.	GOAL	DRAMATIC ACTION	CONFLICT	CHANGE	THEME DETAIL
Chpt.1 SC#1	2/68 Great Divide UFW						

Again, if you would rather continue tracking your scenes, move now to Chapter 6. If you wish to read more about the benefits of research, continue to the end of this chapter.

RESEARCH

Everyone knows that research is critical for historical fiction writers, but I contend that research is crucial for every kind of writing. Not only you, but also your readers, benefit from really knowing what you are writing about. Even if you are writing about a time in which you lived, be it in memoir or fiction form, you cannot rely on memory alone.

If you find yourself lapsing into the use of clichés or, worse, perpetuating the generalizations, prejudices, and over-simplifications we complacently assume every day, delve deeper into the world of your story through research to reveal the truth. If you find yourself stopped by writer's block, plumb the world of your story through research and the block often dissolves.

Stories that tell the truth are firmly grounded in research.

Whenever possible, write your research on Post-it notes and organize your findings on your Scene Tracker.

Research must be woven in artfully.

If your research involves too many details, then indicate on the Post-it notes where to find the files in which the relevant facts and details are located. Be as clear and specific as you can about the information, both on the notes and in the actual files. The creation of a novel can take months and years, and there is nothing as frustrating as coming across an incomplete scribble that makes no sense when you come to that much-needed bit of research.

The use of research is as dicey as the use of flashback that I discussed in the last chapter. Every bit of fascinating information you uncover does not belong in the book unless it contributes to the overall plot, be it the action plotline, the character plotline, or the thematic plotline.

CHARACTER EMOTIONAL DEVELOPMENT

COLUMN 3: CHARACTER EMOTIONAL DEVELOPMENT

Janet Fitch begins *White Oleander* in scene.

> The Santa Anas blew in hot from the desert, shriveling the last of the spring grass into whiskers of pale straw. Only the oleanders thrived, their delicate poisonous blooms, their dagger green leaves. We could not sleep in the hot dry nights, my mother and I. I woke up at midnight to find her bed empty. I climbed to the roof and easily spotted her blond hair like a white flame in the light of the three-quarter moon.

*No iron can pierce the heart
with such force as a period
put just at the right place.*
—Isaac Babel

"Oleander time," she said. "Lovers who kill each other now will blame it on the wind." She held up her large hand and spread the fingers, let the desert dryness lick through. My mother was not herself in the time of the Santa Anas. I was twelve years old and I was afraid for her. I wished things were back the way they had been, that Barry was still here. That the wind would stop blowing.

"You should get some sleep," I offered.

"I never sleep," she said.

SCENE TRACKER — *White Oleander* by Janet Fitch

SC SU	DATES SETTING	CHARACTER EM. DEV.	GOAL	DRAMATIC ACTION	CONFLICT	CHANGE	THEME DETAIL
Chpt.1 SC#1	Nighttime	Deeply identifies with Mo.					
	Santa Ana	12 yrs old Afraid					
		Takes care of Mo.					

ANALYSIS

Scene 1 from Chapter 1 of *White Oleander* is a page and a half. We know it is a scene because the action is being played out moment by moment. Though the narrator says very little about herself directly, we learn several important character emotional development issues about her in this passage:

"We could not sleep in the hot dry nights, my mother and I." This sentence speaks volumes. It shows so effectively how deeply the narrator identifies with her mother.

"I climbed to the roof ..." Again, in showing this action, we understand how connected these two characters are. The child knows from experience just where to find her mother on a night like tonight.

"I was twelve years old and I was afraid for her."

"You should get some sleep," I offered.

PREVIOUS EXAMPLES

1) To continue with our example from Chapter 4, *All the Pretty Horses* by Cormac McCarthy, in Scene 1 there is little to inform us about the protagonist other than his statement at the end of the second paragraph, "You never combed your hair that way in your life, he said." From these simple words, we get the sense that he speaks the truth.

SCENE TRACKER — *All the Pretty Horses* by Cormac McCarthy

SC SU	DATES SETTING	CHARACTER EM. DEV.	GOAL	DRAMATIC ACTION	CONFLICT	CHANGE	THEME DETAIL
Chpt.1 SC#1	Just before dawn	Speaks the truth					

2) To continue with our example from Chapter 5, *The Sea-Wolf* by Jack London, what we find out about the protagonist initially is that he has a tendency to blame others for his misfortunes. In the Summary and Scene 1, we learn that he is intelligent; that he likes to hang out weekly with a man who loafs by reading Nietzsche and Schopenhauer. And that he is a writer.

SCENE TRACKER — *The Sea-Wolf* by Jack London

SC SU	DATES SETTING	CHARACTER EM. DEV.	GOAL	DRAMATIC ACTION	CONFLICT	CHANGE	THEME DETAIL
Chpt.1 SU							
SC#1	Jan. Mon. a.m.	Blames others Intelligent Writer					

Unless I know what sort of doorknob his fingers closed on, how shall I — satisfactorily to myself — get my character out of doors?

— Ford Madox Ford

DEFINITION OF A PROTAGONIST: the hero, or the character who changes the most in the course of the story.

CONTNUE TRACKING

With your Scene Tracker in front of you, refer back to your manuscript and fill in under Column 3 any significant character traits brought forward in your scenes. This is also the place where you indicate any of the important character background information you want to keep in mind about the protagonist.

If you have two major point-of-view characters (two protagonists), or want to track the antagonist as well as the protagonist, just use different colored ink for each of them.

EXPLANATION
The Internal, the Back Story or
Character Emotional Development-Driven Plot

Most popular fiction is 30 percent dramatic (the action plot-line) and 70 percent emotional (the character development).

Even fans of historical fiction who say they enjoy learning about another time and place confess that they read primarily to learn what happens to the characters. Months after having read a story, a reader often cannot recall specific scenes, yet that same reader is likely to remember the growth of the main character.

The character emotional development originates in the back story. The psychological and emotional makeup of characters interests everyone and is why people read fiction in the first place. This is also why your stories, whether they be genre fiction or literary, must focus on the character's emotion.

KEEP IN MIND

Watch for a flaw of your protagonist to come to light in the

Scene Tracker. This will be extremely helpful when we discuss the Character Emotional Development Plotline in the second half of this workbook. For example, is your protagonist a procrastinator, perfectionist? Does he or she act judgmental, greedy, bullheaded, pessimistic, jealous?

At the same time, search for your protagonist's strengths. As much as her flaw creates tension, her strengths and spunk are the attributes that make readers want to stick with her through her problems.

A SUCCESSFUL WRITER writes every single day, even if for only 10 minutes.

CHAPTER

7

GOAL

COLUMN 4: GOAL

In the opening scene of Billie Letts' *Where the Heart Is*, we learn of the protagonist:

> Novalee Nation, seventeen, seven months pregnant, thirty-seven pounds overweight—and superstitious about sevens—shifted uncomfortably in the seat of the old Plymouth and ran her hands down the curve of her belly.

Three paragraphs later the protagonist's scene goal is made abundantly clear:

> But she didn't have sevens on her mind as she twisted and squirmed, trying to compromise with a hateful pain pressing against her pelvis. She needed to stop again but it was too soon to ask. They had stopped once since Fort Smith, but already Novalee's bladder felt like a water balloon.

The difference between a dream and a goal is that a goal is quantifiable.
To achieve your writing goals, make them small and achievable.

SCENE TRACKER — *Where the Heart is* by Billie Letts

SC SU	DATES SETTING	CHARACTER EM. DEV.	GOAL	DRAMATIC ACTION	CONFLICT	CHANGE	THEME DETAIL
Chpt.1 SC#1	In a car headed for CA	17 yrs. old 7 mos. preg. Superstitious about sevens	to use the restroom				

ANALYSIS

Sometimes where a scene begins and ends is not clear-cut and thus the decision becomes subjective. Scene 1 from Chapter 1 of *Where the Heart Is* might be seen as comprising the entire first chapter, fourteen pages. We know it is a scene because the action is being played out moment by moment.

But a dream sequence lies in the middle of Chapter 1, so you might decide that the dream marks the end of Scene 1 and the beginning of Scene 2. Or, the moment Novalee walks into Wal-Mart could be the marker. All this is to say that how you decide where a scene begins and ends is not always an exact science. For our purposes here, it matters less how you decide where a scene begins and ends and more how you justify your decision to yourself for tracking purposes.

Throughout the first fourteen pages of *Where the Heart Is,* we are with Novalee moment by moment. At times, Letts interrupts the *showing* to *tell* us information about Novalee's past. But the telling is always within the context of the action going on in the scene. I make the decision for our purposes here that Scene 1 ends when she enters Wal-Mart.

Either way, Letts establishes Novalee's goal right up front in the scene. This way, tension is created immediately in that the reader knows that something needs to happen pretty soon or Novalee will be in trouble.

PREVIOUS EXAMPLES

1) To continue with our example from Chapter 4, *All the Pretty Horses* by Cormac McCarthy, there is little to inform us about the character's scene goal. Therefore we leave this box blank.

SCENE TRACKER — *All the Pretty Horses* by Cormac McCarthy

SC SU	DATES SETTING	CHARACTER EM. DEV.	GOAL	DRAMATIC ACTION	CONFLICT	CHANGE	THEME DETAIL
Chpt.1 SC#1	Just before dawn	Speaks the truth					

2) To continue with our example from Chapter 5, *The Sea-Wolf* by Jack London, we learn in Scene 1 that the protagonist intends to write an essay titled "The Necessity for Freedom: A Plea for the Artist."

SCENE TRACKER — *The Sea-Wolf* by Jack London

SC SU	DATES SETTING	CHARACTER EM. DEV.	GOAL	DRAMATIC ACTION	CONFLICT	CHANGE	THEME DETAIL
Chpt.1 SU							
SC#1	Jan. Mon. a.m.	Blames others Intelligent Writer	Write essay				

3) To continue from the example from Chapter 6, Janet Fitch's *White Oleander*, we learn of the protagonist's goals in Scene 1:

> *Long-term story goal:*
>
> "I wished things were back the way they had been."

> *Short-term scene goal:*
>
> "You should get some sleep," I offered.

Beware of the trap of talking too much about your story. Instead, use all your energy for the actual writing.
It is possible to kill a story—the punch of it, your passion for it—by talking it to death.

RELAX
BREATHE
TRUST THE PROCESS

For more tips on Goal, go to
www.BlockbusterPlots.com
and click on Plot Tips.

For our purposes of tracking, we mark only the short-term scene goal under Column 4 on the Scene Tracker.

SCENE TRACKER — *White Oleander* by Janet Fitch

SC SU	DATES SETTING	CHARACTER EM. DEV.	GOAL	DRAMATIC ACTION	CONFLICT	CHANGE	THEME DETAIL
Chpt.1 SC#1	Nighttime Santa Ana	Deeply identifies with Mo. 12 yrs old Afraid Takes care of Mo.	Give Mo. comfort				

CONTINUE TRACKING

With your Scene Tracker in front of you, refer back to your manuscript and fill in under Column 4 with the protagonist's goal in the scene.

EXPLANATION
Goals

The short-term scene goals and long-term story goals do not have to be plainly stated, but they do have to be at least implied. A short-term goal gives direction to the scene. Without it, a scene loses its significance and tends to ramble. The protagonist must always be working toward something. Conflict is created by all the factors that interfere with her achieving her short-term scene goals and, ultimately, her long-term goal.

Creating both short-term goals and long-term goals for the protagonist are difficult for many writers. Stick with it. We read to see if the protagonist is going to achieve or accomplish what she wants in life. Suspense is the state of anticipation, wanting to know what happens next.

Often the protagonist's desire rules her entire life only to find in the end, that one's desire does not bring satisfaction. Either way, the goal for you as a writer is to come to know your protagonist well enough to be able to create short and long-term goals for her.

By having the protagonist want something, and that something has to really count to the character, then the reader knows what is at stake.

CHAPTER 8

DRAMATIC ACTION PLOT

COLUMN 5: DRAMATIC ACTION PLOT

The following scene begins Mark Twain's *The Adventures of Tom Sawyer:*

> "Tom!"
> No answer.
> "Tom!"
> No answer.
> "What's gone with that boy, I wonder? You Tom!"
> No answer.
> The old lady pulled her spectacles down and
> looked over them about the room; then she put
> them up and looked out under them. She seldom
> or never looked through them for so small a thing
> as a boy; they were her state pair, the pride of
> her heart, and were built for "style," not service—

she could have seen through a pair of stove-lids just as well. She looked perplexed for a moment, and then said, not fiercely, but still loud enough for the furniture to hear:

"Well, I lay if I get hold of you I'll —"

She did not finish, for by this time she was bending down and punching under the bed with the broom, and so she needed breath to punctuate the punches with. She resurrected nothing but the cat.

"I never did see the beat of that boy!"

She went to the open door and stood in it and looked out among the tomato vines and "jimpson" weeds that constituted the garden. No Tom. So she lifted up her voice at an angle calculated for distance and shouted:

"Y-o-u-u Tom!"

There was a slight noise behind her and she turned just in time to seize a small boy by the slack of his roundabout and arrest his flight.

"There! I might 'a' thought of that closet. What you been doing in there?"

"Nothing."

"Nothing! Look at your hands. And look at your mouth. What is that truck?"

"I don't know, aunt."

"Well, I know. It's jam—that's what it is. Forty times I've said if you didn't let that jam alone I'd skin you. Hand me that switch."

The switch hovered in the air—the peril was desperate—

"My! Look behind you, aunt!"

The old lady whirled round, and snatched her

skirts out of danger. The lad fled on the instant, scrambled up the high board-fence, and disappeared over it.

SCENE TRACKER — *The Adventures of Tom Sawyer* by Mark Twain

SC SU	DATES SETTING	CHARACTER EM. DEV.	GOAL	DRAMATIC ACTION	CONFLICT	CHANGE	THEME DETAIL
Chpt.1 SC#1	Fri. Aunt's house	T: Small smart. fast. liar A: Softy Dead sis's son	Escape	Tom/Aunt trouble			

ANALYSIS

By now you are likely able to easily identify this passage as a scene. The passage is made up of definite action and dialogue and unfolds in such a way that the reader is able to slip into the scene and actually experience the excitement moment to moment.

The passage doesn't indicate the year or season or time of day, but we do know it is Friday and that the scene takes place at the aunt's house.

The first character introduced is Aunt, but since we know that Tom is the protagonist, we write his information under Character Emotional Development first and Aunt's next in a different color.

From the Aunt's monologue, we quickly learn that Tom is a small boy, fast both in mind and on his feet, and that he is a liar.

His goal is to escape.

For the purposes of the Scene Tracker, I abbreviate the action to "Trouble between Tom/Aunt."

Grasp the fundamentals of scene and set your imagination free.

PREVIOUS EXAMPLES

1) Our example from Chapter 4, *All the Pretty Horses,* opens in scene, so there must be action of some sort. The action in the first paragraph is the character entering a house where a dead man is laid out for viewing.

SCENE TRACKER — *All the Pretty Horses* by Cormac McCarthy

SC SU	DATES SETTING	CHARACTER EM. DEV.	GOAL	DRAMATIC ACTION	CONFLICT	CHANGE	THEME DETAIL
Chpt.1 SC#1	Just before dawn	Speaks the truth		View of dead man			

2) To continue with our example from Chapter 5, *The Sea-Wolf,* the dramatic action thus far is limited to the appearance of the red-faced stranger.

SCENE TRACKER — *The Sea-Wolf* by Jack London

SC SU	DATES SETTING	CHARACTER EM. DEV.	GOAL	DRAMATIC ACTION	CONFLICT	CHANGE	THEME DETAIL
Chpt.1 SU							
SC#1	Jan. Mon. a.m.	Blames others Intelligent Writer	Write essay	Stranger appears			

3) To continue with our example from Chapter 6, *White Oleander* by Janet Fitch, the action of the scene primarily revolves around the daughter climbing to the roof to find her mother.

SCENE TRACKER — *White Oleander* by Janet Fitch

SC SU	DATES SETTING	CHARACTER EM. DEV.	GOAL	DRAMATIC ACTION	CONFLICT	CHANGE	THEME DETAIL
Chpt.1 SC#1	Nighttime Santa Ana	Deeply identifies with Mo. 12 yrs old Afraid Takes care of Mo.	Give Mo. comfort	Roof w/ Mo.			

RELAX
BREATHE
TRUST THE PROCESS

4) To continue with our example from Chapter 7, *Where the Heart Is*, the action of the scene is limited to sitting, albeit uncomfortably, in the front seat of a car headed for California.

SCENE TRACKER — *Where the Heart is* by Billie Letts

SC SU	DATES SETTING	CHARACTER EM. DEV.	GOAL	DRAMATIC ACTION	CONFLICT	CHANGE	THEME DETAIL
Chpt.1 SC#1	In a car headed for CA	17 yrs. old 7 mos. preg. Superstitious about sevens	to use the restroom	Driving in a car			

CONTINUE TRACKING

With your Scene Tracker in front of you, refer back to your manuscript. Indicate under Column 5 what action takes place in your scenes. Sum up the action in the scene as succinctly as possible and write that with yet a different color of ink.

EXPLANATION

As I explained in the Flashback section of Chapter 4, story information is generally divided into two parts: the front story and the back story. The front story is all the action that happens in scene on the page as the story moves forward.

The back story is all the history that makes the characters who they are today, why they see the world as they do, and all the history of the circumstances that are unfolding on the page. Back story helps the reader to understand things in context. Back story was discussed in more depth in Chapter 6.

If your story begins with a Summary, there may not be any real action to indicate on the Scene Tracker. Summary is telling and so it does not usually involve real action. However,

Since a scene is not truly a scene unless it has some sort of conflict, tension, or suspense—real or imagined, try to include the pivotal conflict in your description.

Front story is action.

Back story is everything that makes the characters who they are today.

each and every scene involves action, action that moves the front story forward. Action-driven plotline is the front story—the physical events unfolding in a dramatic and exciting way on the page.

CONFLICT

COLUMN 6: CONFLICT

Our example from the previous chapter, the first scene in Mark Twain's *The Adventures of Tom Sawyer*, has conflict. The reader does not yet know that Tom's Aunt is a softy and would never actually use the switch on Tom. So, when she is looking and unable to find him and her frustration grows, the reader anticipates that this mischievous boy is going to get a whipping for not answering her and for hiding out and eating the jam. There is no reason for the reader not to believe her when she threatens: "Well, I lay if I get hold of you I'll—"

By using phrases such as "seize a small boy by the slack of his roundabout and arrest his flight," Twain sets us up to believe that this "small boy" is in for it.

As the story continues, it becomes obvious that the boy is lying:

> "There! I might 'a' thought of that closet. What
> you been doing in there?"
> "Nothing."
> "Nothing! Look at your hands. And look at your

Note the active verbs—seize and arrest. These verbs work on the surface of providing action and also on an implied level of what must be coming.

mouth. What is that truck?"

"I don't know, aunt."

Of course he knows. And the reader knows he knows, and fears for him, knowing that lying can cause dire consequences. Twain goes on to put an actual threat in the mouth of the aunt, and we know disaster is imminent.

"Well, I know. It's jam—that's what it is. Forty times I've said if you didn't let that jam alone I'd skin you. Hand me that switch."

The switch hovered in the air—the peril was desperate—

SCENE TRACKER — *The Adventures of Tom Sawyer* by Mark Twain

SC SU	DATES SETTING	CHARACTER EM. DEV.	GOAL	DRAMATIC ACTION	CONFLICT	CHANGE	THEME DETAIL
Chpt.1 SC#1	Fri.	T: Small smart. fast.	Escape	Tom/Aunt trouble			
	Aunt's house	liar			X		
		A: Softy Dead sis's son					

ANALYSIS

This scene is crafted to keep the reader in suspense by creating conflict on several levels at once. Therefore, an X goes under Column 6, indicating that there is indeed conflict and tension in this scene.

PREVIOUS EXAMPLES

1) To continue with our example from Chapter 4, since *All the*

Pretty Horses opens in scene, not only must there be action of some sort, there must also be some sort of conflict or tension or suspense. This tension is implied by what comes at the end of the action itself. A dead man laid out for viewing creates curiosity or a certain suspense that forces the reader to read on to discover who died and why and what that means to the overall story.

SCENE TRACKER — *All the Pretty Horses* by Cormac McCarthy

SC SU	DATES SETTING	CHARACTER EM. DEV.	GOAL	DRAMATIC ACTION	CONFLICT	CHANGE	THEME DETAIL
Chpt.1 SC#1	Just before dawn	Speaks the truth		View of dead man	X		

2) In our example from Chapter 5, *The Sea-Wolf,* Jack London gives us a hint of what is to come when he closes the first paragraph: "… found me afloat on the San Francisco Bay," and creates curiosity or suspense that forces the reader to read on. Also, whenever a stranger appears, tension is created because the reader wants to know who the stranger is and the part he will play in the story.

SCENE TRACKER — *The Sea-Wolf* by Jack London

SC SU	DATES SETTING	CHARACTER EM. DEV.	GOAL	DRAMATIC ACTION	CONFLICT	CHANGE	THEME DETAIL
Chpt.1 SU SC#1	Jan. Mon. a.m.	Blames others Intelligent Writer	Write essay	Stranger appears	X		

3) To continue with our example from Chapter 6, *White Oleander* by Janet Fitch, not much tension is produced by the action itself since the action of the scene primarily revolves around the daughter climbing to the roof to find her mother. However, throughout the scene the author is setting up the

The best way to improve your writing is through reading.

tone of the story and hits us over and over again with hints and details that foreshadow what is to come. For instance:

> "Only the oleanders thrived, their delicate
> poisonous blooms, their dagger green leaves."
> "Lovers who kill each other now will blame it on
> the wind."
> "I was afraid for her."
> "… that the wind would stop blowing."

The scene continues for another page, and the foreshadowing continues, full of ominous "telling" details, all of which create a sense of doom of what is to come.

SCENE TRACKER — *White Oleander* by Janet Fitch

SC SU	DATES SETTING	CHARACTER EM. DEV.	GOAL	DRAMATIC ACTION	CONFLICT	CHANGE	THEME DETAIL
Chpt.1 SC#1	Nighttime Santa Ana	Deeply identifies with Mo. 12 yrs old Afraid Takes care of Mo.	Give Mo. comfort	Roof w/ Mo.	X		

4) Though the action of the scene in *Where the Heart Is,* our example from Chapter 7, is limited to sitting, albeit uncomfortably, in the front seat of a car headed for California, the author creates tension in the very fact that Novalee is not speaking up for herself and thus is not achieving her goal. The reader reads on, curious as to what is standing in Novalee's way. It does not take long for the reader to learn that Novalee fears the antagonist in this scene, her boyfriend.

SCENE TRACKER — *Where the Heart is* by Billie Letts

SC SU	Dates Setting	Character Em. Dev.	Goal	Dramatic Action	Conflict	Change	Theme Detail
Chpt.1 SC#1	In a car headed for CA	17 yrs. old 7 mos. preg. Superstitious about sevens	to use the restroom	Driving in a car	X		

RELAX
BREATHE
TRUST THE PROCESS

CONTINUE TRACKING

With your Scene Tracker in front of you, refer back to your manuscript and mark under Column 6 with an X if there is conflict or tension or suspense in the first scene of your project. Some writers choose to write a brief summary of the conflict in the box. Remember there is no right or wrong way to use the Scene Tracker. At any time, feel free to adapt it to suit your individual needs.

EXPLANATION

Janet Burroway writes in *Writing Fiction, A Guide to Narrative Craft* that "conflict … is the fundamental element of fiction, necessary because in literature, only trouble is interesting."

Story is conflict shown in scene, and conflict is what makes readers turn the page. Yet one of the most common problems I find with writers in my plot workshops and private consultations is that the conflict in their stories is flat. Or, there's not enough conflict or it's inconsistent. Without some sort of conflict, you do not have a scene or, for that matter, a story.

Conflict does not have to be overt, but it must be there in some form of suspense or of something unknown lurking.

Fill a scene with tension and conflict and you will have yourself a page-turner. Suspense, conflict, and tension make the reader read on. Suspense, conflict, and tension are built through setbacks, not through good news.

Conflict will be covered in more detail in Part Two Plot Planner, but for our purposes here, I want you to determine if there is conflict in the scene or summary you are analyzing. Summary does not always have conflict, which is another reason why you do not want to overuse summary in your stories. Scenes generally have conflict. In Part Two Plot Planner, this will become even more apparent.

TIPS ON CREATING CONFLICT

When deciding on your story problem, use the tension of the action that is unfolding on center stage to be a reflection of the protagonist's internal tension. Be sure to show this internal tension through action and reaction in scene, thereby avoiding too much telling through internal monologue.

A few of the many ways to do this, to heighten the conflict in your story through the use of your character's psychology, are:

1) Show in scene the something or someone your protagonist loves as being threatened. This will force your protagonist to make a decision and act on that decision. Raise the stakes, upping the threat, in the next scene, each time higher than the last "rising conflict."

2) In real life, most of us avoid conflict at all

costs. Women in particular are taught early on to sweep conflict and tension under the rug. Not so in telling stories. People read stories to see how characters grow and change. This change and growth may not be for the better. Change may be for the worse. Without conflict, you do not have a scene. Without scene, you do not have a story. The more tension and conflict you incorporate in your stories, the better. Turn up the pressure on your story characters. Put your protagonist in the middle of what he or she hates the most, then show the choices she makes in her attempt to avoid, change, or escape that which she hates.

3) Show, in scene, your protagonist taking center stage alongside his or her greatest fear.

4) Establish your protagonist's dream. Then "show" him or her constantly sabotaging that dream by the choices made based on his or her character flaw.

By using something within the character's psychology to create tension or conflict you create a multilayered plotline, one involving character growth (the emotional plot) directly linked to the action (the dramatic plot).

For more tips on Authentic Details and Thematic Significance, go to www.BlockbusterPlots.com and click on Plot Tips

The choices the protagonist makes create the action. Both the character and the action will ultimately reflect the underlying theme of your story, the thematic plot. With this sort of interweaving of character, action, and theme, the story you create will be rich in character and conflict, making for a compelling and satisfying page-turner.

CHAPTER

10

CHANGE

COLUMN 7: CHANGE

The opening scene of Kate Chopin's short story, *A Shameful Affair*, begins:

> Mildred Orme, seated in the snuggest corner of
> the big front porch of the Kraummer farmhouse,
> was as content as a girl need hope to be.

(cut to paragraph three)

> From her agreeable corner where she lounged
> with her Browning or her Ibsen, Mildred watched
> the woman [pull the great clanging bell that
> called the farmhands in to dinner] every day. Yet
> when the clumsy farmhands all came tramping
> up the steps and crossed the porch in going to
> their meal that was served within, she never
> looked at them. Why should she? Farmhands are
> not so very nice to look at, and she was nothing of
> an anthropologist. But once when the half

dozen men came along, a paper which she had laid carelessly upon the railing was blown across their path. One of them picked it up, and when he had mounted the steps restored it to her. He was young, and brown, of course, as the sun had made him. He had nice blue eyes. His fair hair was dishevelled. His shoulders were broad and square and his limbs strong and clean. A not unpicturesque figure in the rough attire that bared his throat to view and gave perfect freedom to his every motion.

Mildred did not make these several observations in the half second that she looked at him in courteous acknowledgment. It took her as many days to note them all. For she singled him out each time that he passed her, meaning to give him a condescending little smile, as she knew how. But he never looked at her.

SCENE TRACKER — *A Shameful Affair* by Kate Chopin

SC SU	DATES SETTING	CHARACTER EM. DEV.	GOAL	DRAMATIC ACTION	CONFLICT	CHANGE	THEME DETAIL
SC#1	Lunch Time	A higher class than the farmhands Condescending	To give him a condescending smile	Farmhand crosses class lines	X	+/-	

ANALYSIS

The change column received a +/- because the protagonist's emotion at the beginning of the scene was positive (she was confident and condescending) and ends in the negative (she was being ignored). If the scene had started out with low emotion and had risen as the scene progressed then the change column would have received a -/+.

PREVIOUS EXAMPLES

1) To continue with our example from Chapter 4, *All the Pretty Horses* by Cormac McCarthy, the character shows no emotional change from the beginning of the scene to the end. However, this in and of itself creates tension—we wonder why he feels nothing after having seen the dead man laid out. In showing no change of emotion, McCarthy creates suspense and thus forces the reader to read on to find out why. Later, we learn that the character does not show a lot of emotion and, thus, this opening scene sets the stage for this man who keeps most everything inside.

Therefore, in this example, we leave Column 7 blank.

SCENE TRACKER — *All the Pretty Horses* by Cormac McCarthy

SC SU	DATES SETTING	CHARACTER EM. DEV.	GOAL	DRAMATIC ACTION	CONFLICT	CHANGE	THEME DETAIL
Chpt.1 SC#1	Just before dawn	Speaks the truth		View of dead man	X		

2) To continue with our example from Chapter 5, *Sea-Wolf* by Jack London, the protagonist begins the scene in a confident manner. However, before long the stranger gives the protagonist hints that because of all the fog in the San Francisco Bay, things are amiss:

> He gave a short chuckle. "They're getting
> anxious up there."

Feel free to write the actual change in emotion rather than use the symbols. For instance: she goes from ignoring to being ignored.

Soon after, the boat the protagonist is riding on crashes into another vessel. Fear fills the protagonist as chaos ensues.

SCENE TRACKER — *The Sea-Wolf* by Jack London

SC SU	DATES SETTING	CHARACTER EM. DEV.	GOAL	DRAMATIC ACTION	CONFLICT	CHANGE	THEME DETAIL
Chpt.1 SU							
SC#1	Jan. Mon. a.m.	Blames others Intelligent Writer	Write essay	Stranger appears	X	+/-	

3) In the example I gave in Chapter 6 of the opening scene from Janet Fitch's *White Oleander*, the protagonist's dark mood does not change much throughout the scene. Thus, we leave Column 7 blank.

SCENE TRACKER — *White Oleander* by Janet Fitch

SC SU	DATES SETTING	CHARACTER EM. DEV.	GOAL	DRAMATIC ACTION	CONFLICT	CHANGE	THEME DETAIL
Chpt.1 SC#1	Nighttime Santa Ana	Deeply identifies with Mo. 12 yrs old Afraid Takes care of Mo.	Give Mo. comfort	Roof w/ Mo.	X		

4) To continue with our example from Chapter 7, *Where the Heart Is* by Billie Letts, the protagonist's emotion moves from miserable to hopeful, back and forth from low to high throughout the scene. What is most important here is that Novalee shows emotion and that how she feels at the start of the scene—on the verge of desperation to go to the bathroom—is vastly different twelve pages later when the scene ends. She feels triumphant because not only did she convince her boyfriend to stop, he also gave her enough money to buy herself a pair of shoes to replace the ones that fell through the rusted-out hole

since the next chapter board

SCENE TRACKER — *Where the Heart is* by Billie Letts

SC SU	DATES SETTING	CHARACTER EM. DEV.	GOAL	DRAMATIC ACTION	CONFLICT	CHANGE	THEME DETAIL
Chpt.1 SC#1	In a car headed for CA	17 yrs. old 7 mos. preg. Superstitious about sevens	to use the restroom	Driving in a car	X	-/+/-/+	

5) To continue with our example from Chapters 8 and 9, in *The Adventures of Tom Sawyer* by Mark Twain, we know without being told that the character has a change of emotion from the beginning of the scene, when he is hiding, to the middle of the scene, when he is being threatened with a switch, to the end of the scene, when he runs to freedom. Column 7 receives a -/-/+, meaning that the implied emotion starts out fearful of getting caught to fearful of getting strapped, and finishes favorably.

SCENE TRACKER — *The Adventures of Tom Sawyer* by Mark Twain

SC SU	DATES SETTING	CHARACTER EM. DEV.	GOAL	DRAMATIC ACTION	CONFLICT	CHANGE	THEME DETAIL
Chpt.1 SC#1	Fri. Aunt's house	T: Small smart. fast. liar A: Softy Dead sis's son	Escape	Tom/Aunt trouble	X	-/-/+	

CONTINUE TRACKING

In Column 7, plot the emotion at the beginning of each of your scenes with a plus or a minus sign depending on how the character is feeling at the beginning of the scene. Continue to

RELAX
BREATHE
TRUST THE PROCESS

Keep writing. Do not polish. Do not go back and start over. Keep moving forward. Write your entire book as a rough draft all at once. Do not show it to anyone. Do not worry about spelling or grammar. Just keep writing until you get to the end. Only then do you know what you have.

change the sign as the character's emotion changes.

EXPLANATION

The change in the character's emotion does not have to be significant, but there has to be a change. If not, then the scene has done nothing to develop the character.

Without some sort of emotional change in your character, your story will become stagnant and you will likely lose the reader. Stories are living, breathing organisms. So is your protagonist, who must grow and change as she tries to get something in life and fails and tries again. Each time your protagonist is knocked down, she must get back up and try again.

As long as you are able to record a change in the protagonist's emotional level somewhere throughout the scene, then your chances of keeping the reader's interest increases.

It is best if the protagonist is in worse shape when she ends the scene than when she started the scene. No matter how bad things get for the character, they can and should always get worse.

If you find that your protagonist is always happy or always sad with not many definite changes in emotions, then perhaps you are like the writer who told me that in tracking her scenes she found her piece was "a rather dour story of a dour character." Armed with that realization, she began working on integrating a variety of emotion in some form or another to show more of the protagonist's strengths and hopefulness.

Do not worry if tracking the emotional changes within your protagonist is difficult for you. Most writers have strengths and weaknesses in their writing. For instance, many writers are particularly adept at creating quirky, likable protagonists who feel emotions strongly, but those same authors have difficulty creating dramatic action and lots of conflict. Other writers are just the opposite and can create all sorts of amazing action scenes, but break down when it comes to developing character and emotional development.

Whatever your strengths and weaknesses are, be aware of them. When you are feeling brave and energetic (if, at this point, you were tracking yourself, you would receive a +), spend time in the arena that is the most challenging. When your energy is low (here you would receive a -), stay in your area of strength.

If the -/+ symbols are too confusing for you, just jot down some key words for the emotions. What really matters here is that your protagonist does not remain flat, but that she is emotionally affected by the tension and changes within the scene.

T H E M A T I C   D E T A I L S

COLUMN 8: THEMATIC DETAILS

Carol Shields begins her Pulitzer Prize-winning novel *The Stone Diaries* in scene:

> Birth, 1905
> My mother's name was Mercy Stone Goodwill.
> She was only thirty years old when she took
> sick, a boiling hot day, standing there in her back
> kitchen, making a Malvern pudding for her
> husband's supper. A cookery book lay open on
> the table: "Take some slices of stale bread," the
> recipe said, "and one pint of currants; half a pint
> of raspberries: four ounces of sugar; some sweet
> cream if available." Of course, she's divided the
> recipe in half, there being just the two of them
> and what with the scarcity of currants, and
> Cuyler (my father) being a dainty eater. A pick-
> nibble fellow, she calls him. Able to take his food
> or leave it.

(Cut to paragraph six:)

chapter 11

And almost as heavenly as eating was the making—how she gloried in it! Every last body on this earth has a particular notion of paradise, and this was hers, standing in the murderously hot back kitchen of her own house, concocting and contriving, leaning forward and squinting at the fine print of the cookery book, a clean wooden spoon in hand.

SCENE TRACKER — *The Stone Diaries* by Carol Shields

SC SU	DATES SETTING	CHARACTER EM. DEV.	GOAL	DRAMATIC ACTION	CONFLICT	CHANGE	THEME DETAIL
Chpt.1 SC#1	1905 3:00 July Kitchen	30 years old Passion is cooking	Make Malvern pudding for dinner	Cooking	X	+/-	Stale bread Murderously hot kitchen

ANALYSIS

The opening scene continues for almost six pages, but these paragraphs are enough for our purposes.

The theme is the *why*, your reason for writing the story, what you want your readers to take away. The theme of *Stone Diaries* can be summed up as: beneath the surface of seemingly ordinary women lie extraordinary lives.

Shields opens her story foreshadowing tension by introducing the fact that the mother will take sick. Then, rather than jumping immediately into the cause of the sickness and what happens next, she backs up and by using as ordinary details as one might find—a wife preparing pudding for her husband's dinner and her absolute passion for cooking— Shields effectively introduces the theme and tone of the story to come. She introduces authentic details in the very first paragraph of her story and establishes what her story is about and what it is not about.

Note the Change column. Though Shields begins the scene telling the reader about the mother's illness, when we meet the mother in the next sentence, she is not yet sick. The mother's emotion at the beginning of the scene is positive in that she is doing what she most loves to do—cooking. However, by the end of the scene six pages later, the mother is sick. Therefore, the scene ends in the negative.

PREVIOUS EXAMPLES

1) To continue with our example from Chapter 4, in *All The Pretty Horses* by Cormac McCarthy uses many telling details to bring the scene alive and lend an air of foreboding: "floorboards creaked under his boots," "along the cold hallway," "guttered candlestub," "face so caved and drawn," "the yellowed moustache," "the eyelids paper thin." Although the character shows no emotion, "in the distance a calf bawled."

There are other details, however, that actually enhance the story's theme. That theme is: when a boy is coming of age and the only life he has ever known is disappearing into the past, that boy must leave on a dangerous and harrowing journey to claim his place in the world.

The thematic details are the portraits of forebears only dimly known to him and the death of his grandfather. Both of these details serve as a metaphor for the death of the only life this boy has known.

SCENE TRACKER — *All the Pretty Horses* by Cormac McCarthy

SC SU	DATES SETTING	CHARACTER EM. DEV.	GOAL	DRAMATIC ACTION	CONFLICT	CHANGE	THEME DETAIL
Chpt.1 SC#1	Just before dawn	Speaks the truth		View of dead man	X		Portraits Gr Fa.'s death

> Don't give up on a book until you finish at least the first draft all the way to the end.

If you have not yet discovered your theme, fill in the column with general details and do not worry about the thematic end of things.

2) The theme of our example from Chapter 5, *The Sea-Wolf,* is: through ambition and courage, man is able to survive against all odds. In the first scene, the protagonist ends up in the freezing cold water and fog with only a life preserver. Throughout the latter part of the scene, he shows panic rather than courage over and over again. This is an effective beginning in that the character has room to develop into a man of courage and ambition.

SCENE TRACKER — *The Sea-Wolf* by Jack London

SC SU	DATES SETTING	CHARACTER EM. DEV.	GOAL	DRAMATIC ACTION	CONFLICT	CHANGE	THEME DETAIL
Chpt.1 SU							
SC#1	Jan. Mon. a.m. Writer	Blames others Intelligent	Write essay	Stranger appears	X	+/-	Water like the grip of death Strangled by salt water

3) To continue with our example from Chapter 8, *White Oleander* is a mother/daughter book with the theme of: to find a place for oneself, one must first break away. Although the author does not use any thematic details to illustrate the above theme, she does use ominous details to foreshadow the horror to come: "poisonous blooms" and "dagger green leaves."

SCENE TRACKER — *White Oleander* by Janet Fitch

SC SU	DATES SETTING	CHARACTER EM. DEV.	GOAL	DRAMATIC ACTION	CONFLICT	CHANGE	THEME DETAIL
Chpt.1 SC#1	Nighttime Santa Ana	Deeply identifies with Mo. 12 yrs old Afraid Takes care of Mo.	Give Mo. comfort	Roof w/ Mo.	X		Poison blooms Dagger leaves

4) The theme for our example from Chapter 7, *Where the Heart Is,* is: Home is where the heart is. Novalee's long-term goal is to live in a house, any kind of a house. Up until now "she had never lived in a place that didn't have wheels under it." Therefore, by beginning *Where the Heart Is* in a car, Letts establishes right up front Novalee's reasons for wanting a house. The car is falling apart. A TV tray covers a rusted-out hole the size of a platter in the floorboard.

SCENE TRACKER — *Where the Heart is* by Billie Letts

SC SU	DATES SETTING	CHARACTER EM. DEV.	GOAL	DRAMATIC ACTION	CONFLICT	CHANGE	THEME DETAIL
Chpt.1 SC#1	In a car headed for CA	17 yrs. old 7 mos. preg. Superstitious about sevens	to use the restroom	Driving in a car	X	-/+/-/+	Broken down car Rusted floorboard

5) In *The Adventures of Tom Sawyer,* our example from Chapter 6 and 7, the theme is: There is a collective tendency of man to go overboard toward generosity and forgiveness. Aunt Polly embodies this theme in this very first scene, but there are no real thematic details to illustrate the point. Therefore, we will leave Column 7 blank.

SCENE TRACKER — *The Adventures of Tom Sawyer* by Mark Twain

SC SU	DATES SETTING	CHARACTER EM. DEV.	GOAL	DRAMATIC ACTION	CONFLICT	CHANGE	THEME DETAIL
Chpt.1 SC#1	Fri. Aunt's house	T: Small smart. fast. liar A: Softy Dead sis's son	Escape	Tom/Aunt trouble	X	-/-/+	

**RELAX
BREATHE
TRUST THE PROCESS**

Hang a list of the five senses—smell, hear, taste, see, feel—next to your computer as a reminder to integrate the senses into your scenes.

CONTINUE TRACKING

With your Scene Tracker in front of you, refer back to your manuscript and fill in under Column 7 any and all Thematic Details in each of your scenes.

EXPLANATION

The first time you fill in this column, it is not unusual if you have not worked out the theme of your entire project. For many writers, the theme does not come until the first or second rewrite. Therefore, if you do not have a theme, fill in the column with general details and do not worry about the thematic end of things. Plot any details in the first passage that contribute to the overall meaning of that passage or the entire story. List sights and sounds, smells and tastes, texture and details of your story's setting. List language details true to the time, such as slang and vocabulary. Attempt to use only the details that reinforce the character, the action, and/or the theme of your story.

In the big scenes, try to incorporate all five senses. Sensory details pull the readers into the story in a way that allows them to transcend thinking about your story to feeling it. The sense of smell generally evokes the strongest visceral reaction from your reader. Use details for emphasis but do not overdo them—as in all things, balance is key.

Once you are aware of your theme, go back over the Scene Tracker and mull over each and every detail, searching for inspiration. Sometimes the transformation from a bland or trite or stereotypic detail to an original, specific, authentic one imbued with thematic meaning is easy. Often it is a stretch and involves a shift in perspective.

Imagine your story as a lasting work and attempt to use

specific details that are authentic to the time period in which you are writing. For instance, in the first scene of *Tom Sawyer*, we read: "There was a slight noise behind her and she turned just in time to seize a small boy by the slack of his roundabout and arrest his flight." The roundabout is an authentic and specific detail of the time period in which this story takes place.

By tracking the thematic details in each of your scenes and seeing them hanging on the wall up there in front of you, the Scene Tracker becomes visual proof of how many scenes support your theme and how many stray away from your theme.

As we explore theme, you will begin to have a deeper appreciation of how to more deeply develop theme through details.

In a private consultation, a memoirist related to me the beginning scene of her story with a body lying on the floor with her arms outreached. Though the scene started the story out with a bang, it was bereft of details and thus was not exploited to the maximum. The author did have a theme: Through self-exploration, one is able to reconnect one's divided soul. The body on the floor was the protagonist who was hollow inside but outside she was a comedian, a colorful presence to others. With some plot coaching, the author was able to create a more layered scene by including thematic details of a bright, beautiful painting on the wall and absolutely no furniture, a metaphor for her life.

The change in this example is subtle; there is still no furniture, but by adding the colorful paintings, it shows a deliberate choice in leaving the room stark, not an oversight. Plus, the paintings are in sharp contrast to the emptiness and, therefore, reinforce the theme.

Rather than use clichéd, general, or stereotyped details, research for just the right concrete, definite and specific details.

Write the first draft of your story without thinking about all these details. There will be plenty of time in the rewrites to mull over each and every detail.

Try to always stretch for the most original, authentic details you can.

Janet Fitch, who wrote *White Oleander*, reported that her mentor, Kate Braverman, asked her once what a cliché was. Fitch replied that it was language that had been repeated so often as to be common. Braverman retorted that it is anything you have ever heard, even once. Fitch then set out to write her story using original language, metaphors, and details never before heard.

If you would rather move on with the task of filling in your Scene Tracker, move to Chapter 12 now. If you would like to learn more about theme, read on.

FURTHER READING

A great story weaves together three plotlines: dramatic action, character emotional development, and thematic meaning. Months after readers have finished a great story, though they were turning the pages of the book to learn what was going to happen next in the action or to the character, many cannot call up the action scenes or describe the actual character development. However, even years later those same readers still hold an idea, if vague, of what the story was about or, in other words, the underlining theme of the book.

If you are like me and find theme one of the more difficult aspects of writing to grasp, I suggest that rather than shy away from those things in life that are hard, you walk right into them. Take out your story and roll around in the pages for a few days or more. Stick with it, even if the rolling turns into a temper tantrum of flailing arms and kicking feet and moans of "I don't get it! I hate this stuff!" Feel the fire of uncertainty and insecurity and then go even deeper.

Had enough? All righty then! Stand up and brush yourself off. Close your eyes and take a deep breath. Now another. Open your eyes. Feeling better? My hope is, in putting yourself through the emotional wringer, you might have discovered a theme or two of your life. Since our personal themes generally translate into our writing, perhaps, by going so deeply into your own fears, you have found the energy of your story, the fire, and its theme. Once that happens and you have a sense of the big picture, everything else will follow.

Your reward for doing the hard work is a few easy tips on how to support your themes in your writing. Philip Gerard says in *Writing a Book that Makes a Difference*, that "plenty of strategies are available to the writer for giving greater weight and impact to the theme and connecting more powerfully with the reader." One such strategy is to repeat thematic details. In repeating thematic details you can give emphasis, jog memory, and/or establish rhythm. Let me give you a few examples of each of these.

The Red Tent, by Anita Diamant, is a story of Dinah, a woman only hinted at in the Book of Genesis in the Bible. Let us agree, for our purposes here, that the theme of Diamant's story is that the red tent is where a girl learns what it means to be a woman. The red tent was where women gave birth and were then pampered for a month afterward, the place a girl entered when she began menstruating, and the place she returned every month thereafter. Thus every time the red tent is mentioned or referred to, it gives thematic emphasis to the story.

For a Writers **Plot Planner Workshop DVD** with an emphasis on Thematic Significance, please visit: www.blockbusterplots.com

Search for just the right detail that supports the theme of your project. Use that detail repeatedly, and you will find that each time you do, you will be giving emphasis to your theme.

An example of how the use of repetitions can jog memory is found in Ursula Hegi's historical novel *Stones from the River* which she wrote as an attempt to understand the part of the common man in Germany after the end of World War I and through Hitler's rise to power. Keep in mind that although the detail Hegi uses to jog memory is not specifically a thematic detail, she is reminding us of a character who repeatedly deepens the story's theme through his actions and inactions.

In Chapter 1, Hegi introduces Herr Pastor Schuler with a common and thus universal character trait. "Already he felt the itch of his sweat on his chest and beneath his private parts, a sweat he detested yet was unable to restrain with anything except medicated foot powder that left bone-colored rings on his garments and a chalky trace of dust on the tops of his shoes." In Chapter 3, she repeats this detail: "When Herr Pastor Schuler bent and reached beneath the cuffs of his trousers to scratch himself, Trudi (the protagonist) noticed that the skin on his legs was taut and shiny as though the hairs had all been scratched away. Specks of white powder drifted from under his cassock to settle on the polished black tops of his shoes." Again in Chapter 7: "... The aging pastor, who had been getting thinner over the years as though—by scratching his scaly skin—he were wearing himself away, layer by itchy layer, until soon only his bones would be left." And finally toward the end of Chapter 10, almost halfway through the book, "[the new pastor] wished he could ask the old pastor about [the] confessions, but his predecessor had died the previous year, his poor, scaly shell so dried out that it had barely added any weight to the polished coffin."

Through the use of this scaly skin repetition we are not only reminded of who the man is each time we meet him again on the page. The detail allows us to be there in the moment because all of us can relate to the physical irritation that itchy scaly skin elicits. The author goes to such lengths to reinforce the theme of the story; she wants us to remember this man over the course of the first half of the book because she uses his actions to "show" how, little by little, he and the other villagers made concessions as Hitler became more powerful, until there was no turning back. It is precisely this simple detail of scaly skin that drives home the idea that, if such a man as a pastor could fall prey to such human failings, then could such a thing happen to the very people we know and love? And, ultimately, this forces each of us to ask if we could have made those same small concessions?

In the same story, Hegi repeatedly uses a monthly chess game to which Trudi's father had belonged since he had been a boy, one that had been going on for four generations. In this example, the use of repetitions establishes a sort of rhythm to the story while reinforcing the theme.

> "The men would take the chess sets from the birch wardrobe, sit down at the long tables, and play, their silence punctuated only by punched chess clocks and the clipped warning: "Schach" —"Check." The white tablecloths would ripple, stirred by the rhythm of restless knees. Gradually, as it got warmer in the room they would take off their jackets and sit there in their suspenders."

The chess game Hegi uses dramatically sets a thematic rhythm throughout her story and becomes yet one more example of how she "shows" through the changes in this one ritual, that had been virtually unchanged for generations, how life in this small town was tragically deformed by the onset of World War II.

Do not simply rely on memory or random personal experiences. Research for just the right details.

Ask yourself if you can come up with an authentic detail specific to your story, yet universal, so when it is repeated, it draws the readers in and allows them to "be there" in the story. And, at the same time, try to make it reinforce your theme.

I chose these examples of such brilliant use of thematic details in repetition with the firm belief that they came to their authors just like yours will come to you, through a lot of hard work and many rewrites. The search for just the right thematic detail will ensure that each new rewrite you undertake will give your story a sharper focus and greater depth. Even better, these sorts of thematic threads make the struggle to identify the themes you live your life by, and thus your story's theme, worth the effort.

F I N A L   A N A L Y S I S

CREATING A LASTING TAPESTRY

Congratulations! You have begun the process of plotting out
your scenes on the Scene Tracker. Granted, the Scene Tracker
represents merely one half of the entire process (Part Two
follows), but even so, what you have begun is a substantial and
important commitment to your writing.

For those of you who started out kicking and scream-
ing that this sort of methodical, organized approach to writing
is counterproductive to the creative process and not for you, the
fact that you are reading this passage says to me that you walked
into your fear. The reward for doing that which you most resist
is always life changing. Congratulations!

Now, continue to fill in the Scene Tracker one scene at
a time until you arrive at the last date, last action, final character growth or regression, and the last perfect thematic detail of
your story. At first, you may need to refer back to the scene
tracker explanations often. Be patient. In time and with practice, the elements of scene will become integrated into your
being and seem second nature to you.

If, however, tracking each and every scene slows you
down or becomes too tedious, adapt the techniques in any way

CHAPTER 12

Trust the process.

Most writers find that by plotting things out on the Scene Tracker with everything so visual is helpful in terms of looking at the elements of scene in detail.

These are merely guidelines. The intent is for you to vary the design in anyway that best supports your story. If everyone did it exactly the same we'd have a bunch of cookie-cutter stories instead of unique works of fiction.

that best works for you and use that. Remember, this process is intended to support you in your writing.

> One writer confessed that "using the Scene Tracker was exhausting (emotionally and physically)—an hour or two of toxic colored-pen fumes and shoulder aches from writing on the wall. But when I was finished and could stand back and look at my chart, I was exhilarated. There's really so much in my story—funny episodes, sadness, courage, the craziness of the 1960s. I was too close to see all the elements until I charted it out. That's what I liked the best about the Scene Tracker: it enabled me to organize and make some order out of chaos."

ANALYSIS

Now, sit back and examine your Scene Tracker. See if you can discover the mysteries and gems that you were unable to detect when you were blinded by your words and phrases, paragraphs and pages of narration. The Scene Tracker shows you one of the structures of your story. Part Two Plot Planner will show you another.

Search the Scene Tracker for any gaps or holes you can tighten, any leaps you made in the characters' progress, or any failure that needs to be smoothed out step-by-step throughout the course of the story. Make notations on the Scene Tracker with Post-it notes to remind you to cut that which is not contributing to the whole or to flush out that which you skimmed over the first time around.

Continue reading for an idea of how to decide which

scenes to cut and which ones to rework and which ones to keep. Emotional change and conflict are the two most critical aspects to good fiction and, though they are most commonly missing in the early drafts of a story, it is possible to go back and crank up the tension and conflict and create more emotional change in subsequent drafts.

Once you have your Scene Tracker in shape, if what you find there inspires you to begin one of the countless rewrites that are in store for all fiction writers, go for it. At any point you lose your passion for the actual writing, move on to Part Two Plot Planner.
Good luck!

For those of you who examined your Scene Tracker and decided that what you need is an actual re-visioning of your project, do not despair. The answers are right there in front of you; they are always lurking in our stories. Part Two Plot Planner will help you locate them.

In Part Two Plot Planner, you will learn how to plot your scenes and how to best maximize cause and effect. You will learn how to develop a compelling character plot line with lots of emotional changes. You will learn how to create exciting and dramatic action full of tension and conflict in your action plot line. And you will deepen your understanding of the importance of theme from your thematic plotline.

After completing both Part One Scene Tracker and Part Two Plot Planner, you will be ready to use all of the techniques to create a richly detailed and complex tapestry, a tapestry with

In every case, where a scene has a blank box under Change or under Conflict, rethink those scenes.

Track the 7 most important elements of a scene on a Scene Tracker for your own individual project with the Scene Tracker Kit.
http://www.blockbusterplots.com

Every narrative has a multitude of possible scenes from which to choose.

Writers who are detached from the stories they write seem better able to finish a short story, memoir, creative nonfiction or full-length novel with fewer rewrites.

a bold border and compelling body, a resilient heart, and an expansive spirit. And once this complex fabric is woven with words and images, you might just find yourself holding a blockbuster novel.

SCENES TO CUT, THOSE TO KEEP

A skill that defines a good writer is the ability to know which scenes to keep and which ones to kill. By creating a Scene Tracker and a plotline for your story, you can better select those scenes that best advance the story you've been chosen to write and those scenes that, in the interests of the story, should be reduced to summary or—dare I say it? Cut out completely.

Likely you've noticed that I wrote, "...the story you've been chosen to write." Before you roll your eyes and dismiss this line as another of my "out there" concepts, I would like you to take a moment to consider the reason I have included such a seemingly preposterous idea.

When we as writers honor a story as something beyond ourselves, we put distance between our egos and that which the story needs. In other words, rather than falling in love with certain passages or sentences or characters or plot turns that they've spent hours laboring over, these detached writers appreciate those aspects purely for the sake of the story itself.

A good writer knows that for a certain passage or sentence or character or plot turn to work in a story, it is not the beauty of the writing or the cleverness in the plotting or the depth of the characters that is crucial, although these things are important to captivate the reader. A good writer knows that each line and each element in each scene belongs there because it has a definite purpose in the overall scheme of things.

Make your scenes work for you by incorporating a

strand of each of the plotlines into every scene. Pretend there are three doors in every scene, one for character emotional development, one for dramatic action, and one for thematic significance. Open each door, one by one. For example: Door 1—What aspect of the character is developed in this scene? Door 2—Where is the tension? Door 3—How has the theme of the story been advanced?

A good scene progresses the dramatic action, the character emotional development, or the thematic significance. The truly great scenes do all of it at once. I guess I should continue on that vein and say that any scene that does not do several of these key functions at once does not belong in the story. With your Scene Tracker in hand, evaluate your story honestly. Where are the holes in the logic of your story? Where do your characters come up shallow and weak? Where does the thematic thread break? If you cut the scenes with no tension and the scenes with no emotional change, is the story better off without them? Yes? Then for the sake of the story, you know what you need to do. If you see yourself as the steward of the story, you will yield to the flow of the story and do what is right. If you see yourself as the creator, then you will resist the elimination of any scenes, period. The choice is yours.

If you choose to do what is right for the story and ultimately what is right for your readers, go ahead and weep over all the time and effort you have just cut out of the story. When you are finished moaning and wailing over the unfairness of it all, dry your eyes. You have made the choice to be a good writer. The story and your readers will thank you for putting the story first.

The ability to view the narrative as a separate entity, apart from ourselves, allows us to more effortlessly cut those scenes.
This skill saves us time and heartache, and ultimately makes us better writers.

PLOT PLANNER

INTRODUCTION

PLOTTING IS LIKE JUGGLING

Imagine yourself as a juggler. Start by using one ball. For our purposes, we will label this first ball Dramatic Action.

Now, try tossing this first ball into the air. It is best to "pop" the ball from the palm of your hand rather than let it roll off your fingertips. This also applies to plotting out your stories. It is best to start out with a "pop" of Dramatic Action rather than to let things roll along at a leisurely pace. Also, it is best not to start by throwing the ball too high. And from one scene to the next, try for smooth transitions; do not let the action drift.

With the Dramatic Action ball in play, it is time to integrate ball two. This one we will mark as Character Emotional Development. As the action ball starts on its way down, pop the Character ball in the air. That means that when the tension or conflict or suspense caused by the Dramatic Action starts to fall or lose its effect, use your character's emotional development, his or her flaw or prejudice or fears to cause more.

What message do you want your reader left with after reading the story? This will be ball three, Thematic Significance. Each ball or element of plot sends the others airborne.

As you become confident with these three balls, add more—the subplots of secondary characters, history or politics, and so on. The more you practice, the better you will become until you are tossing the balls while standing on one foot with your eyes closed. Eventually you may even be able to juggle knives and mallets and the kitchen sink.

Like a juggler, the more adept you are at keeping all three elements of plot rising and falling through cause and effect, the deeper, richer, and more compelling your story.

PLOT PLANNER

THE PLOT PLANNER is a visual tool to help you keep an eye on your story as a whole as you work on its parts.

Make whatever adaptations you need to encourage you to actually do the work.

Practice in and of itself will not turn all of us into jugglers. Some of us do better when the steps are mapped out on paper. In the case of plotting, think of the Plot Planner as the route or map of the journey you envision for your protagonist. Along this route, the three elements of plot will rise and fall – the Dramatic Action, Character Emotional Development and Thematic Significance.

When you start planning your plot, your route is likely to be sketchy with lots of gaps and dead ends, but these will be smoothed over and filled in as you come to know your story and characters better,

Once the plan is in place and you and your protagonist set off together, one of you is likely to trip up or misread the map or even intentionally veer off the planned route. Stay loose, but try to keep close as the Dramatic Action sends your character off a cliff or crashing through the underbrush to slay a dragon or two before fighting her way to the top peak. Puffing hard, you reach the summit together. Oops, it's not the summit after all. A crisis ensues. The true summit shimmers in the distance. In a rush of energy and excitement, you scramble alongside your character toward the final struggle, the climax of the book.

Just as with the Scene Tracker, I recommend building your Plot Planner on big pieces of banner paper. Instead of the banner paper running up and down like the Scene Tracker, the Plot Planner runs horizontal. The two together take up quite a bit of space on the wall, but both pieces serve as a continual visual reminder of the entire project. This helps you keep the larger picture always in your mind as you concentrate on smaller parts, writing and rewriting chapters and scenes, creating just the right sentence, choosing just the right word.

If you do not have the space available or simply are not inclined to wallpaper your walls with story ideas, then use smaller paper. Or, if you are adept at keeping all these ideas in your head at once without the visual support, go ahead and do this on your computer. Find a way that works for you.

Again, there are no rules when it comes to writing fiction. Every idea I present to you has as many exceptions as the rule. Every Pulitzer Prize-winning example I present can be matched by Pulitzer Prize-winning example of an author who did just the opposite. The ideas of scene and plot I put forward in *BLOCKBUSTER PLOTS Pure and Simple* are guidelines that have helped hundreds of other writers.

Now that you have completed Scene Tracker, you are ready to develop the actual story map in Plot Planner.

SHOW UP.
TRUST YOURSELF.
TRUST THE PROCESS.

PLOT
DEFINITION

PLOT:
WHAT IS IT?

> This is an example of what plot is NOT: The king
> dies. The queen dies.
> This is an example of what plot IS: The king dies
> and then the queen dies of grief.

EXPLANATION

Sure, the first example tells the reader what happens and the telling carries a certain dramatic flair in that it involves death. On a stretch, we call this Dramatic Action. But remember the juggling example in the last chapter? The trick is to keep three balls or plotlines rising and falling at once. In the first example, there is Dramatic Action, but no Character Emotional

Development. No Thematic Significance. Furthermore, the king dies, the queen dies is episodic. There is no linkage between the two events, no cause and effect.

The king dies, and then the queen dies of grief demonstrates plot. The Character Emotional Development is that the queen's grief over the king's death kills her. Extract from that the Thematic Significance: love kills. Lastly, the two events demonstrate cause and effect, because they are linked by causality. In other words, the king's death is the cause, and the queen's grief—and ultimate death—is the effect.

DEFINITION

> Plot is a series of SCENES that are deliberately arranged by CAUSE AND EFFECT to create DRAMATIC ACTION filled with TENSION and CONFLICT to further the CHARACTER'S EMOTIONAL DEVELOPMENT and provide THEMATIC SIGNIFICANCE.

WHAT DOES THAT MEAN?

I know this definition is complicated. But before you throw up your hands in frustration, stop and study the words that have been capitalized.

I. SCENES

Plot is a series of SCENES …
All your scenes and summaries are marked on your Scene Tracker.

II. CAUSE AND EFFECT

Plot is a series of scenes that are deliberately arranged by CAUSE AND EFFECT …

All but one of the key words in the plot definition have already been identified and indicated on your Scene Tracker.

CHAPTER 6 covers Cause and Effect in more depth.

For now, Cause and Effect means that each scene comes directly out of the scene that came before it. In other words, one scene causes the next scene. This creates a satisfying story to readers, because each scene is organic. By that, I mean that from the seeds you plant in the first scene, the next scene emerges.

III. DRAMATIC ACTION

Plot is a series of *scenes* that are deliberately arranged by *cause and effect* to create DRAMATIC ACTION ...

Your Scene Tracker holds a snippet description of the Dramatic Action for each of your scenes. The dramatic meaning comes from the action scenes, the scenes that are played out moment by moment on the page through action and dialogue.

CHAPTER 7 gives a plan for the Dramatic Action of your piece.

IV. TENSION AND CONFLICT

Plot is a series of *scenes* that are deliberately arranged by *cause and effect* to create *dramatic action* filled with TENSION and CONFLICT ...

You know which scenes are filled with Tension and Conflict just by glancing at your Scene Tracker.

CHAPTER 7 gives you a visual idea of how Tension and Conflict affect the overall plot of your story.

V. CHARACTER EMOTIONAL DEVELOPMENT

Plot is a series of scenes that are deliberately arranged by *cause and effect* to create *dramatic action* filled with *tension and conflict* to further the CHARACTER'S EMOTIONAL DEVELOPMENT.

Emotional meaning always comes from your characters. Character Emotional Development is indicated on your Scene Tracker scene–by–scene.

CHAPTER 8 shows how Character Emotional Development interweaves with the Dramatic Action.

CHAPTER 22 gives you techniques to explore Thematic Significance.

VI. THEMATIC SIGNIFICANCE

Plot is a series of *scenes* that are deliberately arranged by *cause and effect* to create *dramatic action* filled with *tension and conflict* to further the *character's emotional development* and create THEMATIC SIGNIFICANCE.

The Thematic Significance ties your entire story together. It is the reason you wrote your story, what you hope to prove by writing your story.

If you are one of the lucky ones, you know the theme of your piece. You have already begun developing the Thematic Significance of your piece through the use of just the right details, and these details are marked on your Scene Tracker.

If the Thematic Significance of your story eludes you for now, you do have marked on your scene tracker an idea of the details available to expand and exploit when the theme makes itself known to you.

LAYERS OF PLOT

Beyond the different layers of plot we just went over, you can also plot out other aspects of your story: the setting, the history, the politics, and the weather. However, in this book, we will only concern ourselves with the layers we just outlined; the others you are free to explore when you conceptualize your plot.

RELAX

We are getting ahead of ourselves here. Breathe. Remember, the harder you try to get this, the harder it is for the information to penetrate your brain. Stand up. Shake out your hands. Roll your head. Better? Trust the process. You are going to get this, just like you got Part One Scene Tracker. Think not? Have I let you down so far?

PLOT
PLANNER

THE FORM

What I am about to show you is a visual plotting tool that many writers, myself included, have found helpful in plotting out fiction, memoirs, and creative nonfiction: the Plot Planner. The Plot Planner helps explain plot. It also helps create a plot. The Plot Planner displays a vision of your project. See it as a bridge between the invisible world of creativity and the visible world of the five senses.

Before you actually copy the Plot Planner onto your piece of banner paper, read through the following background and explanation. Chapter 15 will take you through the actual creation of your Plot Planner.

THE BEST PREDICTOR FOR SUCCESS is not talent alone. The best predictor of success is the amount of deliberate practice you are willing to commit to for your project's completion.

Every story has its own energy.

For information about a private plot consultation on your individual project, visit: www.blockbusterplots.com

There are two options:

Either

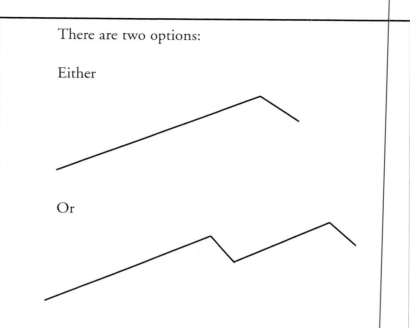

Or

When I started teaching plot intensives, I described the design of the Plot Planner as waves cresting. Typically, the structure of a short story builds to one giant wave in which the crisis serves as the story's climax. Novels, memoirs, and creative nonfiction often have two peak moments, the second one being the climactic moment. In this case, the crisis and the climax are written as separate scenes. Again, there are no rules. Use whatever format best supports your story. The description that follows incorporates all the component parts. Vary and revise them as you will.

EXPLANATION

The flow of each story emanates from Dramatic Action, Character Emotional Development, and Thematic Significance. The Chinese call this flow in humans *qi* (pronounced "chi"). The *qi* directs and coordinates the flow of energies, and is the mainstay of one's life-force. *Qi* cannot be touched or seen, but it is inherently present in all things.

Within the form of your story, the energy rises and falls like a "wave" undulating in an up and down movement.

SIX STANDARD ANTAGONISTS

Man Against Man: family, friends, coworkers, enemies, lovers.

Man Against Nature: hurricanes, earthquakes, floods, natural law, physical disabilities such as deafness or blindness, physical and mental illness.

Man Against Society: religious institutions, government, customs, gangs.

Man Against Machine: cars, robots, space ships, motorcycles. (In science fiction, the machines
generally are taking over.)

Man Against God: spiritual beliefs.

Man Against Himself: inner life, past mistakes, fears, flaws, doubts, moral choices, will.

A story is the shifting of power back and forth between the protagonist and the antagonist.

Story is about struggle.

A protagonist pushes toward something, while forces internal and external attempt to thwart her progress. In each of the Six Standard Antagonists, the struggle is between the protagonist, Man, who wants something enough to take action against all odds and against all the antagonists or forces within and without the protagonist who work against her.

The Plot Planner is merely a line that separates the scenes into those where the energy or power is with the antag-

onist (above the Plot Planner line) and those where the protagonist is in control or holds the power over the antagonist
(below the Plot Planner line).

ABOVE THE LINE

Like the surface of the sea with its white caps and waves and
swells, the external, gripping territory of the Dramatic Action
when your protagonist is out of control, fearful, lost, confused,
or under the power of an antagonist as the story unfolds moment
– by – moment belong above the line. All scenes that show complications, conflicts, tension, dilemmas, and suspense go above
the line. Any scene that shows action where the power is somewhere other than with the protagonist goes above the line.

BELOW THE LINE

Below the line is where the mystery lies. Scenes that belong below
the line are all the scenes that show the undertow, the internal,
emotional territory of the protagonist. Much of the Character
Emotional Development ends up below the line, because character development often is revealed through character introspection.
Any scenes that slow the energy of the story or in which the power
shifts back to protagonist belong below the line.

Notice that the Plot Planner line is not flat. The line
moves up steadily higher. The swell builds slowly and method-
ically. The stakes of the story rise higher and higher. Tension
builds. Each scene shows more tension and conflict than the
one that came before. Each defeat the character suffers is more
intense, more costly, as the story progresses.

STRUCTURE

A novel can usually be divided into three parts: the beginning,
the middle, and the end. Remember, however, that rules are

The scenes where the power
is with the **ANTAGONIST** go
above the Plot Planner line.

The scenes where the power
is with the **PROTAGONIST**
go **below** the Plot Planner
line.

The stakes of the story
rise higher and higher.

made to be broken.

I. PART ONE: THE BEGINNING

Part One begins on Page One. Estimate how many pages your story has and divide by four. That is the page number where Part One: The Beginning of your story ends and the next part begins. Most writers are the strongest in the beginning. Many find it easy to write seventy-five pages of compelling scenes, but struggle to keep the momentum going beyond that point.

THE BEGINNING of your story usually commands about a quarter of the energy in the overall project.

II. PART TWO: THE MIDDLE

The middle is the longest portion of the project and commands the most scenes. This is where many writers come up short. Daunted by the long expanse that awaits them, they stop in despair.

    Then they begin another story. Part Two generally ends soon after the character reaches the false summit on her mountain journey, the crisis.

THE MIDDLE of your story usually commands a solid half of the energy in the overall project.

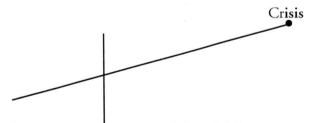

The Beginning   **The Middle**

THE CRISIS

The Crisis is the point where the energy of the story is at its highest point so far. If you are writing a short story, this may remain the highest point. In short stories, generally speaking, there need be only one high point.

THE CRISIS is where the tension and conflict peak.

In facing the greatest fear or pain or disappointment or most unexpected shock or betrayal or failure, the protagonist is forced to see herself clearly for the first time. In some cultures, this time is referred to as the dark night of the soul. It is a turning point. Will the protagonist ignore the wake-up call? Or will the protagonist grow and change as a result of the Crisis?

In a novel, once the protagonist has been hit with the Crisis, the story is not over. The Crisis is actually the false summit. Once there, the true summit becomes visible. The dip in the Plot Planner is where the energy of the story drops, giving the reader time to breathe after the excitement of the Crisis, before undertaking the journey to the Climax.

III. PART THREE: THE END

Subtract a quarter of the pages from the entire page count. This is where the end generally begins.

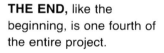

THE END, like the beginning, is one fourth of the entire project.

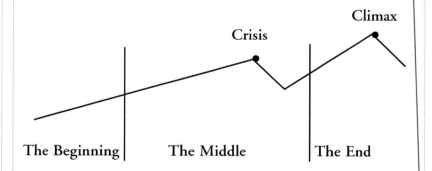

The End is made up of three parts (as most everything in your story has three parts—a beginning, middle. and end.) The end is the buildup to the Climax, the Climax itself, and the Resolution.

THE CLIMAX

The Climax is similar to the Crisis in that it is another point of high drama. But if the protagonist is given a chance to view herself clearly during the Crisis, the Climax is that protagonist's opportunity to show if she has indeed changed. After the Crisis, the protagonist might say with full conviction that she will never be the same. But it is one thing to say it and quite another to actually do it. At our core, all of us have a natural tendency to resist change, preferring to hold tight to the comfort of the familiar. To stretch and grow and change involves the unknown. Rather than risk the possibility of failure, most of us would rather not even try. The Climax involves some sort of action that forces the protagonist to show the reader who she is at her core.

Old habits are tough to break. A person, or a character put in a high-conflict, high-tension situation will first fall back to the old ways. The suspense increases. The reader knows the protagonist has sworn he or she has changed. Will he or she act accordingly?

THE ENERGY of your story has been building scene by scene and now, at the Climax, it reaches a crescendo.

RESOLUTION

Not all of the subplots need to be resolved by the end of the story, but the important ones do. Tie up only enough so that you provide thematic meaning to your overall project.

THE RESOLUTION is where you tie up loose ends.

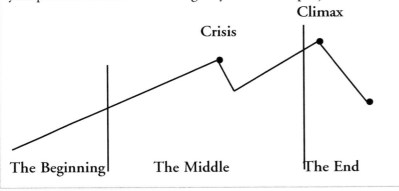

Crisis   Climax

The Beginning   The Middle   The End

PLOT PLANNER PARAMETERS

THIS ENTIRE CHAPTER IS OPTIONAL.
If you benefit from fixed, concrete guidelines for determining the breakdown of what scenes belong in the formation of The Beginning, The Middle, and The End of their plotline, read on.
If you'd rather let your intuition decide, move to Chapter 16.

DETERMINE PARAMETERS

A Plot Planner is divided into Part One: The Beginning; Part Two: The Middle; and Part Three: The End. Before you construct a Plot Planner for your project, it is best if you are able to determine the parameters of each part.

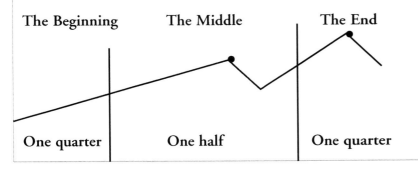

An average novel sold in bookstores consists of sixty scenes. Keep in mind that this is an arbitrary number.

BY SCENE

Refer to your Scene Tracker. Count the number of scenes you have written. Do you envision more or less upon completion? If you have not yet started a project, choose any number of scenes based on how you see your story.

_____ **Total number of scenes.**

Now divide the total number of pages of your book by four to determine the number of pages for each of the three parts of your book (If there are only three parts, then why divide by four, you ask? You will see shortly the logic behind this.)

I. PART ONE: THE BEGINNING SCENES

The Beginning portion of your Plot Planner encompasses approximately one-quarter of the total scenes. Thus, if you have sixty scenes, the Beginning portion has fifteen scenes. How many scenes are in the Beginning portion of your project?

_____ **Beginning # of scenes**

II. PART TWO: THE MIDDLE SCENES

The Middle portion of your Plot Planner encompasses approx-imately one-half of the total scenes. (This is why you divide by four—the Middle is twice as long as either the Beginning or the End.) If you have sixty scenes, the Middle portion has thirty scenes. How many scenes are in the Middle portion of your project?

_____ **Middle # of scenes**

III. PART THREE: THE END SCENES

The End portion of your Plot Planner will encompasses approximately one-quarter of the total scenes. If you have sixty scenes total, the End portion holds the final fifteen scenes. How many scenes do you envision your story having in the End portion?

_____ **End # of scenes**

There is another way to determine the parameters of your plotline that is based on the number of pages in your book. If you are happy with the numbers you choose in this first section, move on to Chapter 16. If analyzing the page count to determine the parameters better suits you than the scene count, keep reading.

You are able to determine the parameters of your plotline by scenes or by page numbers. You decide.

BY PAGE COUNT

From an informal survey of an insider's magazine on the publishing business, _Publishers Weekly_, the average length of a novel is about 250 to 300 pages. That average length of 250 to 300 pages translates to between 60,000 and 90,000 words. A historical novel can run up to 500 pages or more. Keep in mind that the longer the book, the more expensive to produce. Your readers are the ones who end up paying those higher costs.

If you have a rough draft finished, determining the length of your book should be pretty simple. If you have just started a project, estimate the length you envision for the final product based on a similar book to yours you admire.

_____ **Total pages**

Now, you will use the same process that you did for the scenes. Divide the total number of pages of your book by four to determine the number of pages for each of the three parts.

I. PART ONE: THE BEGINNING PAGE COUNT

The Beginning portion of your Plot Planner will encompass approximately one-fourth of the total page count. Using an example of 300 pages total, the Beginning portion equals seventy-five pages. How many pages do you envision your story in the Beginning?

_____ **Beginning # of pages**

II. PART TWO: THE MIDDLE PAGE COUNT

The middle portion of your Plot Planner will take up approximately two quarters of the total page count of your project. Using the example of 300 pages total, the Middle portion of the Plot Planner equals 150 pages. How many pages do you envision in the Middle portion of your project?

_____ **Middle # of pages**

For more tips on the Plot Planner Parameters, go to www.BlockbusterPlots.com and click on Plot Tips

III. PART THREE: THE END PAGE COUNT

The End portion of your Plot Planner will encompass approximately one-fourth of the total page count. Using an example of 300 pages total, the End portion equals seventy-five pages. How many pages do you envision in the End portion?

_____ **End # of pages**

Okay, with all these numbers you have a pretty good idea where Part One: The Beginning of your story begins and ends; where the longest part of the project, Part Two: The Middle, begins and ends; and where Part Three: The End begins and ends.

TAKE A BREAK

You did not know you were going to have to do math to plot out your project, did you? This is it, I promise. You will use the numbers you generated here in the actual construction of your Plot Planner, but after that, no more numbers! And remember, these numbers are simply guidelines.

Before we move to the actual construction of your Plot Planner, why not get up and make yourself a cup of tea? All that mathematical work can give some of us a big fat headache. So, sit back with your tea and look over your numbers. See your story in your mind. Take a deep breath. Invite in a spirit of discovery. Trust the process.

C O N S T R U C T   Y O U R
P L O T   P L A N N E R

GETTING STARTED

To start, retrieve your SCENE TRACKER, the numbers you generated in Chapter 15, and another piece of banner paper.

Adapt the ideas to stimulate a feeling of excitement, expectancy, and enthusiasm. The looser you stay, the easier it is for discovery to flow. Confidence and joy create a safe atmosphere from which to explore.

Again, as I mentioned in Scene Tracker, if, at any point, you are motivated to write, put the plotting aside and write.

I. THE BEGINNING

The form is divided into three parts: Part One: The Beginning, Part Two: The Middle, and Part Three: The End. We will begin at the beginning.

There is no right or wrong to what I am offering here. These are some ideas that have helped other writers. I offer them up to you so that you do not have to go it alone.

At the very heart of this book lies the intention to support you in your writing.

The Beginning portion of your book ends with a scene of high intensity and meaning.

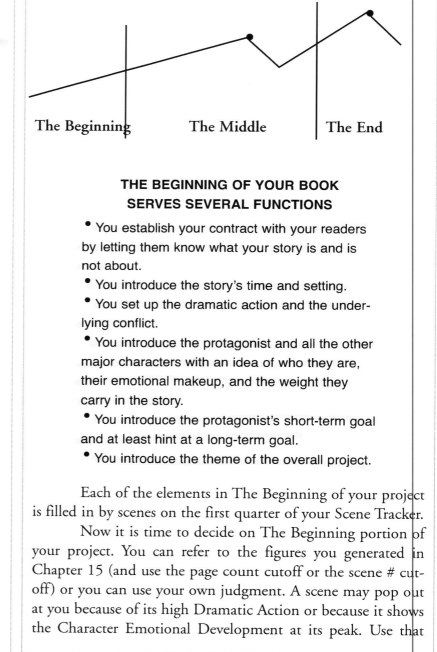

The Beginning   **The Middle**   **The End**

THE BEGINNING OF YOUR BOOK SERVES SEVERAL FUNCTIONS

- You establish your contract with your readers by letting them know what your story is and is not about.
- You introduce the story's time and setting.
- You set up the dramatic action and the underlying conflict.
- You introduce the protagonist and all the other major characters with an idea of who they are, their emotional makeup, and the weight they carry in the story.
- You introduce the protagonist's short-term goal and at least hint at a long-term goal.
- You introduce the theme of the overall project.

Each of the elements in The Beginning of your project is filled in by scenes on the first quarter of your Scene Tracker.

Now it is time to decide on The Beginning portion of your project. You can refer to the figures you generated in Chapter 15 (and use the page count cutoff or the scene # cutoff) or you can use your own judgment. A scene may pop out at you because of its high Dramatic Action or because it shows the Character Emotional Development at its peak. Use that one to end the Beginning portion of your Plot Planner, even if the scene is either a bit before or a bit after the numbers you came up with in Chapter 15.

The parameters we set up in Chapter 15 are meant only as guidelines. It is not necessary to follow those figures exactly. For now, decide where you believe the Beginning portion of your story begins and where it ends. Now turn back to your Scene Tracker and draw a black line from left to right after the scene that ends Part One: The Beginning. All the scenes that come before that black line—The Beginning portion of your story—are the ones you will plot out on your Plot Planner.

TAKE ACTION
PLOT PLANNER FORM
PART ONE: THE BEGINNING

Position the butcher paper so it lies horizontal on the table in front of you. Expose only part of the paper, just a couple of feet, for now. Draw a line, starting about one-quarter of the way up the paper, and make the line so it sweeps steadily upward.

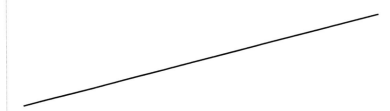

There. That is all there is to creating your Plot Planner Form for The Beginning of your story.

Review your scenes from the Beginning portion of your story to see that they meet the functions listed on page 128.

**RELAX
BREATHE
TRUST THE PROCESS**

PLOT THE BEGINNING

THE BEGINNING

In Chapter 14, we went over the different sorts of antagonists, one or more of which your protagonist faces in your story. (Remember, the protagonist is the character who is most changed by the end of the story. The antagonist is who or what stands in your protagonist's way of achieving her goal.)

1. Man Against Man
2. Man Against Nature
3. Man Against Society
4. Man Against Machine
5. Man Against God
6. Man Against Himself

Now, it is time for you to decide which scenes in The Beginning portion of your story belong **ABOVE THE LINE** of your Plot Planner and which scenes go **BELOW THE LINE**.

The scenes with high energy and vitality go above the line.

ABOVE THE LINE

The scenes where the dramatic action shows an antagonist controlling or holding the power over the protagonist go above the line. For instance, if Scene 1 has the protagonist prevented from doing something she desires because of her insecurity, then the antagonist (Man Against Himself) is in charge, and that scene goes above the line.

DRAMATIC ACTION

Scenes that show Dramatic Action involving the following:

Tension	Conflict
Suspense	Catastrophe
The Unknown	Betrayal
The Chase	Deception
Vengeance	Rebellion
Persecution	Rivalry
Conspiracy	Unnatural Affection
Criminal Action Toward the Protagonist	Suspicion

belong *above the line* of the Plot Planner.

CHARACTER EMOTIONAL DEVELOPMENT

Scenes that show Character Emotional Development involving:

Loss	Failure to Cope
Revenge	Self-Sacrifice
Loss of Control	Anger
Poor Decision-Making	Grief
Criminal Action by the Protagonist	Fear
Rebellion	Greed
Unhappiness	Out of Control
Thwarted by Personal Flaw	Loss of Power

also belong *above the line* of the Plot Planner.

BELOW THE LINE

Scenes in which the protagonist is in control belong below the line. These scenes are necessary to show Character Emotional Development or to give the reader a chance to take a breath after a particularly Dramatic Action. But at their core, these scenes lack power and vitality. Too many of them in a row, and you will put your reader to sleep.

If the protagonist in Scene 1 is in charge of things, or at least not particularly threatened in any way, then Scene 1 *goes below the line*.

DRAMATIC ACTION

Scenes that involve either of the following:
- a lull in conflict, tension, and suspense,
- a sharing of information with the reader by
  telling rather than showing,

belong *below the line* of the Plot Planner.

CHARACTER EMOTIONAL DEVELOPMENT

Scenes in which the protagonist is:
- Calm
- Coping
- Solving Problems
- In Control
- Planning
- Introspective
- Contemplative

belong *below the line* of the Plot Planner.

Note: Refer to Appendix 1 for a visual representation of these elements.

Begin the story above the line with some sort of tension or unanswered question and your reader will immediately be drawn into the story.

EXAMPLE

In *Where the Heart Is* by Billie Letts, the protagonist is Novalee, seventeen years old and seven months pregnant and superstitious about the number seven. In the first few scenes, the antagonist is her boyfriend, Willy Jack.

The book opens in scene with Novalee and her boyfriend on their way from Oklahoma to California. Novalee needs to stop to use the bathroom, but they have already stopped once for the very same reason, and Novalee knows it is too soon to ask again. Tension mounts as her bladder causes her more and more discomfort and, eventually, pain. Because there is tension in the scene, and because Willy Jack holds the power, not Novalee, Scene 1 goes above the line.

WJ refuses

The Beginning

The more scenes that go above the line in the beginning pages of your story will help ensure your readers commitment for the duration.

In the next scene, Novalee awakens from a dream to find that her shoes fell through the rusted-out hole in the floorboard of the car. Willy Jack agrees to stop at a Wal-Mart store. After Novalee uses the bathroom, she buys some rubber thongs and receives $7.77 in change. She runs outside to find the car and Willy Jack gone.

This scene, Scene 2, also goes above the line. Why? Because although Novalee starts the scene in control of things, the scene ends in disaster.

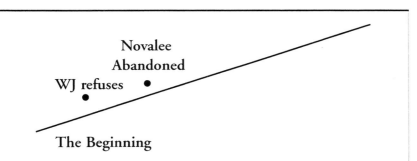

In the next several scenes, Novalee meets three people, each of whom will play a part in her life as the story progresses, though we do not know this at the time. Not much happens in these scenes. This is a risky thing to do so early on; we are only on Page 17. Usually, the Beginning portion of a project is where a writer keeps things moving to entice the reader into the dreamscape of the story. However, in this case, slowing down works because there is so much tension hovering over the story.

The fact that Novalee is pregnant, in the middle of nowhere, and has only $7.77 creates enough tension and suspense to carry these quieter scenes.

The reader flips the pages to learn how this young girl is going to take care of herself. Each time Novalee meets someone, the reader waits for her to ask for help and each time Novalee keeps quiet, the tension builds ever higher.

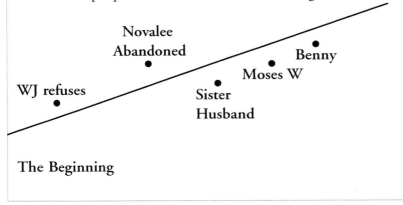

To receive free monthly plot tips and inspiration, contests and events, please visit: www.blockbusterplots.com

Any sort of looming unknown makes it possible for you to slow things down without the fear of losing your readers.

One of the best tricks to keep in mind is that if the protagonist is in worse shape at the end of a scene than at the beginning, you—as the writer—are in good shape. The emotion of the scene is constantly changing and the tension remains high.

RELAX
BREATHE
TRUST THE PROCESS

EXPLANATION

If you are like most writers, you generally find that The Beginning scenes are the easiest to come up with. Perhaps after you listed them on your Scene Tracker, they needed a bit of work, but you were able to find enough conflict and tension and good Character Emotional Development to make you feel confident. As you plot these same Beginning scenes on the Plot Planner, you might be pleased to find that the tension generated in The Beginning scenes rises, and a nice flow in the cause and effect is revealed.

Also, please note, that the line of the Plot Planner is not straight, but climbs steadily higher. This is because the tension does not stay the same, but climbs steadily higher in each and every scene. Much more is at stake in Scene 10 than in Scene 1.

Novalee is sympathetic because she is at her core a good person attempting to do the right thing. She is also a survivor. This is important. The protagonist of a story cannot be passive. As the tension and conflict continue to rise, the protagonist has to be able to pick herself up off the floor time and time again. No matter how bad things get, find a way to make them even worse.

TAKE ACTION
BEGIN PLOTTING THE BEGINNING

With your Scene Tracker next to you and your Plot Planner in front of you, decide which of your scenes go above the line and which ones belong below the line. If your first scene has tension and conflict, or the power is with someone or something other than the protagonist, jot above the line on the Plot Planner the shorthand you created for Scene 1, e.g. Novalee abandoned, from the Dramatic Action column of your Scene Tracker.

If there is no tension or conflict in Scene 1, then the scene notes belong below the line.

Move to the next scene. Does Scene 2 go above or below the line? Write it in. Continue this way, moving down the Scene Tracker until you come to the solid black line. Once you are finished with the scenes in the Beginning portion of your book, stop and take a look at how your scenes are arranged on the Plot Planner.

If most of your scenes are above the line, you are assured that there is enough Dramatic Action to keep your reader turning the pages to find out what happens next. If, however, you find most of your scenes below the line, you could be in trouble. There is no rule for how many scenes belong above versus below the line. However, if too many scenes in a row are below the line, it could mean that your story is too passive, too flat, or that there is not enough excitement for the reader, not enough tension or conflict.

Many scenes that belong below the line are filled with internal monologue and, thus, are inherently non-dramatic with little action. Internal conflict is essentially non-dramatic in that it cannot be played out moment–by–moment on the page. Do not get me wrong. Internal conflict is essential for depth. But dramatic action makes the scene; scene makes the story.

KEEP WRITING

If the activity above stimulates in you ideas and answers for your story, go back to the actual writing. Whenever you lose the energy for writing, continue to show up each day, but instead of turning on your computer, turn to your Scene Tracker or

You do not want to find too many scenes below the line, especially not too many in a row.

My intention is to expose you to guidelines that work so that when you break them , you are doing so deliberately to achieve a specific result.

Plot Planner and this book and continue to mine your scenes and plot your action and character development. Dig for answers. Dig for depth.

PLOT BY CAUSE AND EFFECT

Plot is a series of scenes arranged by CAUSE AND EFFECT to create dramatic action filled with tension and conflict to further the character emotional development and create thematic significance.

CONGRATULATIONS!

You have begun the process of plotting out your story. Now, before we test the scenes for cause and effect, I want you to sit back and take a few minutes to examine The Beginning portion of your Plot Planner.

How many scenes were you able to plot above the line? How many scenes are below the line? Were you honest about the scenes you put above the line? Do they indeed have some sort of tension and conflict? Does the power reside with someone other than the protagonist? Yes? Terrific! Still not sure? That is okay. As long as you can justify in your own mind why you put them where you did, that is enough for now.

Episodic events and random incidents are either boring or disconcerting.

CAUSE AND EFFECT

> Plot is a series of scenes that are deliberately arranged by CAUSE AND EFFECT ...

What Does That Mean?

Cause and Effect is a critical element to plotting out your novels, short stories, memoirs, or creative nonfiction.

Cause and Effect means that the events that happen in one scene cause the events that happen in the next scene. If you are able to link your scenes by cause and effect, each scene is organic. By that, I mean that from the seeds you plant in the first scene grow the fruits of the next scene.

EPISODIC

Let me give you an example of what is NOT cause and effect. Say you are looking at the arrangement of the scenes in your story. Do you find yourself saying, this (whatever it is) happens first and then this happens next and then this happens next and then.... You get the picture. If you ever hear an agent or editor tell you that your story is "too episodic" or "not linked enough," this is what is meant.

CAUSE AND EFFECT

When you plot a story by deliberately arranging a series of events by cause and effect, you will not be told your work is too episodic. To test if your story is tight and if your scenes are arranged by cause and effect, see if you can go from scene to scene saying, "In this scene, this (whatever it is) happens. <u>Because</u> that happens, then this happens and <u>because</u> of that happening, then this next conflict arises."

Do you notice the rhythm? What you planted in the

first scene emerges in the next scene. The second scene cannot happen without the first scene happening first. The third scene happens, <u>because</u> the first two scenes unfolded before it. Each element is linked.

We are always striving to find meaning in the bigger picture. We want to know why one thing leads to the next—to feel the inevitability of cause and effect. Your readers will expect that the events that unfold in one scene will have repercussions in the next.

When you find a scene in your story that does not arise from the scene that comes before it, see if you can, without shifting the focus of the scene, at least introduce an element designed to lead into the next scene in a sentence or two. For instance, say that the theme of the story is: the answers are always right there in front of you. If Scene 1 ends with the protagonist staring into a telescope, Scene 2 starts with the protagonist dusting or moving the telescope. This technique is not as satisfying as true cause and effect, but it at least provides a sense of continuity in non-related scenes.

If you find that even this strategy of linking scenes through chosen details does not work, then you may need to cut that scene or tweak it in such a way that it becomes the effect of the scene that comes before it. You cannot stick a scene in your story just because the writing is beautiful or the format intriguing. You owe it to the reader to provide meaning.

Think of conflict in scene as the cause. The character's reaction to that cause is the effect the conflict has on the character. When the character responds to the conflict, that creates yet another cause and, in turn, another effect follows. The story then moves from scene to scene by cause and effect. Every part plays into the whole, and you end up with a satisfying story.

Scenes are episodic if they are NOT linked by cause and effect. If scenes are linked by cause and effect, each scene is meaningful to all the other scenes.

EXAMPLE

From the example we used in Chapter 17, *Where the Heart Is* by Billie Letts, we can go from scene to scene and find cause and effect well established and in place.

For instance, because Willy Jack refuses to stop, Novalee is forced to ask him, yet again, to stop. Because Novalee keeps asking Willy Jack to stop, he abandons her. Because he abandons her, Novalee ends up meeting Sister Husband, Moses W. and Benny.

Because each scene is linked to the one that came before it and the one that comes after, we draw a line from one to the next to indicate that the connection is unbroken.

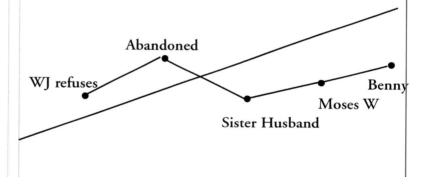

TAKE ACTION

Ready to take a look at the scenes you plotted from the Beginning portion of your story? Okay, it is time to test if your story is tight and if your scenes are arranged by cause and effect.

Start at Scene 1. Say to yourself, "In Scene 1, this (whatever it is) happens." Now ask yourself, "Does what happens in Scene 1 cause Scene 2?" Yes? Then draw a line linking Scene 1 to Scene 2. No? Make a note to yourself either way.

RELAX
BREATHE
TRUST THE PROCESS

Now move to Scene 2. Again, ask yourself if what happens in Scene 2 causes the conflict or action in Scene 3?

Move from scene to scene, asking yourself if one scene causes another. Each time you find cause and effect taking place, draw a line from one scene to the next to indicate the linkage between the two. Continue this way until you arrive at the end of the Beginning portion of your story.

Do not worry if every single scene does not flow from cause and effect. This is just a guideline, as is every other technique I offer you in this workbook. A working knowledge of cause and effect helps to ensure that you are creating a satisfying story structure. The more adept you are at creating cause and effect, the better.

If you find that, in most cases, the story flows naturally from one scene to the next through cause and effect, you are in good shape. If you find that, in most cases, the story is more episodic, then you will benefit from further exploration into the aspect of cause and effect.

Note: Please refer to Appendices 3 & 5 for examples of scenes from The Beginning portion of two more novels plotted out by Cause and Effect.

PLOT THE CHARACTER EMOTIONAL DEVELOPMENT

PLOT is a series of
scenes
arranged by
cause and effect
to create
dramatic action
filled with
tension and conflict
to further the
*character's
emotional
development*
and create
thematic significance.

Plot is a series of scenes that are deliberately arranged by cause and effect to create dramatic action filled with conflict to further CHARACTER EMOTIONAL DEVELOPMENT …

Most popular fiction is 30 percent dramatic action and 70 percent emotional character development.

With the help of *Where the Heart Is* by Billie Letts, I

will take you through a technique that helps deepen a story's overall plot by using Character Emotional Development.

CHARACTER GOALS

Your protagonist (for that matter, all your characters) has an immediate goal for every scene and an overall story goal. These goals help to develop the front story, the story that is unfolding moment –by– moment in scene.

Remember the pattern of scene we established in Part One Scene Tracker? A mini-plot of goal, conflict, and disaster makes up a scene (similar to the overall plot structure of a story). Each scene needs an immediate goal.

In *Where the Heart Is,* Letts alludes to Novalee's immediate goal in the first paragraph of the book, and then establishes in Paragraph 7 that her immediate goal is to use a bathroom.

This simple goal works because Novalee is desperate. She is seven months pregnant and her bladder is "like a water balloon."

The author goes on to establish the long-term, overall goal for the entire story at the top of Page 5—to live in a house like the pictures she collects from magazines. Novalee's mother walked out on her when she was seven years old and she has never had a home that was not on wheels.

Sometimes, the long-term, overall story goal is something the protagonist dreams of having. Dreams are things we wish for, things we enjoy thinking about, but not necessarily things we can attain. Goals come from dreams. Goals are under our control; they are quantifiable and measurable. Dreams involve a bit of magic.

For instance, if your goal is to finish your book,

Your protagonist's goal for each scene is already listed on your Scene Tracker.

For more examples of how to create a **Plot Planner**, please visit: www.blockbusterplots.com.

you can do specific things toward making that happen, all of which are under your control. However, if your dream is to be published, a bit of magic is needed. An agent and/or an editor need to become entranced by your story. The marketplace must be ready for your product. The stars must be aligned to make your dream come true.

Short-term goals are specific things your protagonist has decided she needs to accomplish within a clearly defined period of time. The protagonist's long-term story goal may, in fact, be more a dream than a goal.

CHARACTER FLAW

The protagonist's goals set up the action for the scene. Tension is immediately established, because the reader has something to worry about. Will the protagonist achieve her immediate goal? Is she scene –by –scene, chapter –by –chapter, getting closer to achieving her overall story goal? By now, you know that the more obstacles you toss in the path of the character's journey, the more tension and conflict you create in a scene.

Therefore, what better way to achieve conflict and tension than to craft something that stands in the way of her immediate goals?

One way to do this is to have the character act toward her goal, and then to have something inside of herself (or the people in her life or the outside world or all of the above) react in a way that blocks her success.

In *Where the Heart Is*, Willy Jack stands in the way of Novalee's immediate goal by refusing to stop so she can use the bathroom. Her success is blocked. Tension is created. Now it is

An effective means for creating tension is with a character flaw that will constantly get in the way of the protagonist achieving her scene goals.

up to Novalee to decide what to do next.

However, something inside the character can block her own success. One technique to create a roadblock in the protagonist's journey toward her goal, short term and overall—can be the protagonist's character flaw.

Novalee's character flaw is that she does not speak up for herself. As soon as Willy Jack abandons Novalee, we witness her inability to ask for help. This is a powerful deterrent toward her meeting with success.

To create tension and conflict, the goal must be important to the protagonist. She must stand to lose something if she is not successful. There needs to be some sort of risk involved. For Novalee, if she is not able to stop soon to relieve herself, well, you know what will happen next. Yet, even though we know what she needs in the first paragraph of the story, out of fear of angering Willy Jack, she does not speak up until Page 6.

Novalee's character flaw of not speaking up for herself takes on universal appeal, because it is a common flaw that many people share.

EXAMPLES OF FLAWS

Drinks too much

Judgmental

Spends too much money

Gambles

Lies

Worries too much

Gossips

Procrastinates

Violent temper

Cheater

Unfaithful

The protagonist must be drawn as a complex individual with both strengths and weaknesses.

Or pick one of your own flaws—we all have them—and then exaggerate it.

CHARACTER STRENGTH

To offset the protagonist's flaw, she must also have strength. A protagonist cannot be passive; she must have some character strength to give the reader at least a hint that she is capable of, if not overcoming her flaw, at least of becoming conscious of it.

Story is struggle and so the protagonist must have the strength to fight against all odds and brave conflicts. Every time the protagonist's will has been overwhelmed, she must gather her strength and fight back.

Novalee is intelligent and kind. She is tough, and more than anything else, she is a survivor.

HATES

It is best if the protagonist feels strongly about things. The emotion of hate carries with it a great deal of energy. Hate creates drama and conflict and tension, which are the building blocks of fiction and memoir. Hate gives the protagonist direction, gets her going, moves her, invigorates her, revs her up, brings her to life, gives her power and strength.

Novalee hates people feeling sorry for her, which is why she does not speak up for herself.

LOVES

For a reader to sympathize with your protagonist, your character must show that she has feelings. Something in life must make her happy or bring her satisfaction. By showing that your

For more tips on Character Emotional Development, go to www.BlockbusterPlots.com and click on Plot Tips

You want your readers to feel an affinity and affection for your protagonist.

Fear is a powerful way to create tension and suspense.

protagonist cares about something, your reader will better be able to empathize with her. By establishing what the protagonist loves and then by threatening that thing or person, the protagonist is forced to move. Sparks fly.

Novalee loves babies and nice people. But most of all, she loves taking pictures. Photography was her favorite class in high school. Letts establishes this love in the first four pages of the book. This love ends up playing a major role in the overall plot.

FEAR

All of us are afraid of something. By establishing fear in your protagonist, you create a thread of universality. There are many kinds of fear: fear of failure, fear of responsibility, fear of the unknown, fear of the dark. Fear generally paralyzes us, which is why your protagonist needs to embody all the other emotions. That way the reader is assured that the protagonist will in fact react.

In *Where the Heart Is*, Novalee fears her boyfriend. This sets up tension on the first page of the book.

EXPLANATION

The protagonist's emotions and psychology give depth and meaning to your story.

Go back to The Beginning scenes you plotted out in Chapter 17. Mark the scenes that show the Character Emotional Development. Over the duration of the story, the character will develop from one who is unconscious of her flaws and strengths to a fully actualized (or at least more conscious) protagonist.

When we arrive at the Middle portion of your story, I

**RELAX
BREATHE
TRUST THE PROCESS**

will show you how to develop more tension at the crisis by using the protagonist's flaw. When we arrive at the End portion, I will show you how to use the protagonist's flaw to deepen the climax.

TAKE ACTION
FILL OUT THE FORM
CHARACTER EMOTIONAL DEVELOPMENT

Following is a form to fill out for your protagonist; it also helps if you fill one out for the villain, or antagonist. This way the antagonist, if it is a person, will be a three-dimensional, interesting character rather than a flat cliché. Do one for each secondary character and discover more angles to develop.

As you fill out the form for your protagonist, wait before you jot down your answers. What comes to you first may be superficial. In waiting and inviting the protagonist in, a deeper more compelling answer may come to you.

Note: Please refer to Appendix 4 for an example of a completed form.

CHARACTER EMOTIONAL/PSYCHOLOGICAL PLOT INFORMATION

Protagonist's name:

Overall story goal:

What stands in his/her way?

What does he/she stand to lose, if not successful (risk)?

Flaw or greatest fault?

Greatest strength?

Hates?

Loves?

Fears?

Secret?

P L O T   T H E   M I D D L E

PART TWO: THE MIDDLE

The Middle portion of your book comprises approximately one-half of all the scenes in your entire project. It is where the main action of your story takes place. This long, empty expanse often appears daunting, like a huge wasteland waiting to devour you, the writer. The Middle has stopped many good writers in their tracks.

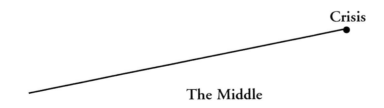

Crisis

The Middle

Many writers leave The Beginning on a high note and launch off into The Middle. You and your characters have now crossed into the heart of the story world. You continue show-

CHAPTER 20

The Middle is especially difficult for all writers in light of our rule of creating rising conflict.

ing up day after day. You come up with some bumps along the way that interfere with the protagonist's progress. Your page count doubles. Things are going great. You feel confident and excited.

And then boom! Somewhere in the middle of The Middle, your confidence turns to doubt. You begin to flounder.

At this point, if you are like other writers, you are desperate to return to the place of discovery. To ease your way out of the terror of the unknown, you ignore the mantra of doggedly continuing to the bitter end and instead go back to the start of the story and begin again. You rationalize that just as soon as you incorporate all those loose ends, you will be better prepared to persevere to the end.

Yet inevitably, when you arrive at the stopping point, you flounder yet again. Sound familiar?

Rather than rip the Scene Tracker and the Plot Planner off the wall and stuff them in the bottom of the file cabinet, I am here to encourage you to keep at it. I know you believe there must be a fatal flaw in your story. That is not necessarily so.

I bring up the difficulty of the Middle not to frighten you, but to prepare you. After all, your attitude directly affects your energy as you write, which, in turn, affects the energy of your project. The last thing I want is to send your energy spiraling downward. I bring up the difficulty of the Middle because it has stopped too many good writers.

I bring up the negatives so that you understand that when you hit the brick wall, it is not you. It is the nature of the beast.

EXPERIMENT

A writer in one of my workshops once asked a fellow writer to stand up and hold out his arm sideways with his thumb pointing down. Then she instructed him to resist when she pressed down on his arm. He was able to keep his arm steady against the pressure.

Next, she asked him to think about something negative concerning his writing. This time, using the same pressure, his arm gave way, as if he had lost all his strength. Then, she asked him to concentrate on a positive experience or feeling. He was easily able to resist the pressure on his arm.

This experiment shows how negative emotions, like worry and doubt and criticism, affect our physical energy. It also illustrates the strengthening effect that positive thoughts and emotions have on us physically.

I mention this experiment to encourage you to stay positive. Take a look at all the scenes you have plotted out on the Plot Planner. Do not see the Scene Tracker or the Plot Planner as half empty. See them as half full. The direction of your focus does not change the reality of the holes and gaps that are on your Scene Tracker and your Plot Planner, but your attitude certainly changes your energy and enthusiasm to persevere.

TAKE ACTION
CONTINUE PLOTTING
THE MIDDLE

It is the time to create The Middle portion of your Plot Planner.

DETERMINATION AND PERSEVERANCE are two key traits of successful writers. Stay determined. Persevere all the way to the end of your project. Until you reach the end, you will never truly know what you have.

RELAX
BREATHE
TRUST THE PROCESS

The Middle portion of your book is twice as long as either The Beginning or The End.

Retrieve your Scene Tracker, the numbers you generated in Chapter 15, and the Plot Planner you have already begun.

On your Scene Tracker, start at the black line that denotes the end of The Beginning and count down the number of scenes that you decided upon for The Middle. Take a look at where that puts you in the story. If that place in your story does not feel like the best stopping-off place for The Middle, look on either side of it. Does another scene pop out at you for its high Dramatic Action? Is there a scene where the Character Emotional Development is at its peak? We are looking for the highest point of tension and conflict in the story so far. Find one? Use that to end the Middle portion of your Plot Planner, even if the scene is a bit before or after the numbers you came up with in Chapter 15. Draw a black line from left to right on your Scene Tracker after the scene that ends Part Two: The Middle.

The parameters we set up in Chapter 15 are guidelines only. It is not important to follow them exactly. For now, decide where you believe The Middle portion of your story begins and where it ends.

Roll out twice as much banner paper for The Middle as you did for The Beginning.

Continue the line you started for plotting, making it sweep steadily upward. About six inches from the end of this portion of the banner paper, drop the line down about half a foot.

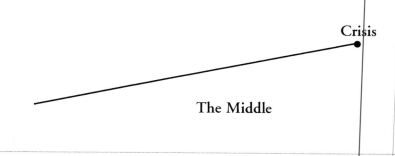

There, that is all there is to creating your Plot Planner Form for The Middle of your story.

Start plotting your scenes.

A TIP

One trick to developing scenes for the Middle is to use some unique task or job or setting for the front story action. Readers like to learn new things when they read. For instance, many of the middle scenes of *The Secret Life of Bees* by Sue Monk Kidd involve the world of beekeeping. Within the context of the plot, the reader learns all sorts of details about bees and honey. Similarly, *Balling the Jack* by Frank Baldwin is filled with inside information into the world of high-stakes dart games. E. Annie Proulx in *The Shipping News* sets her story in a remote location that many readers may never have considered—the Newfoundland coast. She fills her scenes with details of the world of shipping and tides and newspaper writing.

CRISIS

You will notice that the long desertlike wasteland of the Middle culminates at a high point. This is the Crisis, the highest point of tension and conflict in your story thus far. It is this point, the Crisis, that serves as a beacon to guide you through the Middle.

Each scene in the Middle portion of your story marches the protagonist one step closer to the Crisis. The protagonist believes she is marching closer and closer to her long-term story goal, so when she gets to the Crisis, she may be shocked. The

The Crisis is the dark night of the soul.

Do not fall into the trap beginning writers often make. Never summarize where a scene is needed.

reader, however, has experienced the steady march and feels the inevitability of this shocker from the linkage between each scene and the constantly rising tension of story.

It is only in the darkness of a crisis in our lives—a failure or the loss of a loved one or the breakup of a marriage or the termination of a treasured job—that we are forced to see ourselves as we truly are. Toward the end of the Middle portion of your story, you want your protagonist to be confronted with her basic character flaw in such a dramatic way that she can no longer remain unconscious of her inner self.

This creates the key question: in knowing her flaw, will the protagonist remain the same or be changed at her core? You know as well as I do that in the heat of battle we say all sorts of things in our attempt to scramble back to our comfort zone. We make pacts with whatever power we believe controls our destiny. We promise to never be so foolhardy or curious or judgmental or angry or whatever your protagonist's flaw is so long as we are able to go on, survive, make it past this horrible situation that has triggered such a life changing wake-up call.

Of course, it is quite another thing to actually follow through on all those promises, once life settles down. We will not worry about that, yet. For now, all you need to do is to create a scene that puts the protagonist in such an uncomfortable, potentially life-threatening or ego-threatening situation that she has to finally see herself for who she truly is.

Of course, because the Crisis is such a turning point in the story, and fraught with tension and conflict and suspense, it has to be written in scene.

If you find yourself quickly summarizing events, instead of creating the Crisis, stop and ask yourself: am I shying away from this because the material seems too hard, too long, or too painful to write? If the answer is yes to one of these, take a deep breath and try writing the events moment by moment. You may find yourself crying or perspiring or swearing at the screen in front of you as you write. Do not give up. Keep at it. Dig deep. Use the emotion.

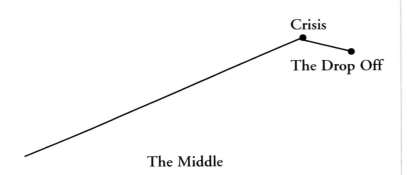

As you will note, after the Crisis, the Plot Planner line drops for the first time. This is because after the intensity of the Crisis, you want to give your readers an opportunity to rest for a moment, to digest all that has gone on thus far. This is a time for both your reader and your protagonist to reflect on things. This is a quiet time after the crisis, a happy time. It can not be all struggle. As with the other parts of your story, the resting cannot go on for too long.

For more tips on Plotting the Middle, go to www.BlockbusterPlots.com and click on Plot Tips

PLOT THE END

THE FINAL LEG OF THE JOURNEY

The fact that you survived The Middle, whether you limped your way through it or leaped over the obstacles and the unknowns, is cause for celebration. Go ahead. Beat your chest and proclaim to the world that you made it!

THE FALSE SUMMIT

When your character reached the Crisis, she thought everything was over—until, that is, she caught a glimpse of the even higher mountain still quite a distance away. That is when she realized she was only at the false summit. So, how do you and she make it to that next peak, the true summit? Step-by-step, just like you made it to the Crisis.

As I said in the last chapter, we make pacts with what-

As unbelievable as it might seem, you are in the home stretch, the final third of your story.

In your first draft, work to get it all down on paper and to survive. Subsequent rewrites you can become more creative.

ever power we believe controls our destiny. Your protagonist does the same thing. She promises to never be so foolhardy or curious or judgmental or angry or whatever her flaw is, so long as she is able to go on, survive yet another day, make it past this horrible thing that has triggered such a life-changing wake-up call, the Crisis. Yet, once life settles down to normal, and the fear has vanished, the conflict gone, somehow we forget our promises. Your protagonist likely does the same thing. Now, it is time we address this universal character reaction.

THE TRUE SUMMIT

Your protagonist has been confronted with an uncomfortable, potentially life-threatening or ego-threatening, situation and finally sees herself for who she actually is. Now she has to make a decision. Is she going to rationalize her way out of change, shoving her promises to a dark corner of her mind? Or, does she accept the challenge to move from her comfort zone and risk the unknown to live her life differently for evermore? You decide. Or let your protagonist decide. Whatever the answer, it is up to you, the writer, to create scenes in this final part of your story that will allow the protagonist to make choices, whereby "showing" the reader which direction she is going to go.

You, as the writer, get to decide if your protagonist will beat the odds and succeed in being changed forever. The only way to show that is by creating scenes that give the protagonist the opportunity to make choices. Although this is the final third of the story, you have one-quarter of the total number of scenes and one-quarter of the total number of pages of your entire book in which to do this.

TAKE ACTION
CONTINUE PLOTTING
THE END

Now is the time to create Part Three: The End portion of your Plot Planner.

To start, retrieve your Scene Tracker, the numbers you generated in Chapter 15, and the Plot Planner you have already begun.

The scenes that belong in The End portion of your project are all the scenes that are left on your Scene Tracker after the second black line. Because you did not necessarily adhere to the parameters we set up in Chapter 15, the number of scenes left may or may not equal the final quarter of the total scene count. That is fine. For now, just decide where you believe The End begins.

Expose only the part of the paper you will be working on for now. Continue the line you have started, making it sweep steadily upward from the drop-off point. Bring it to the highest peak thus far and then drop the line down about half a foot.

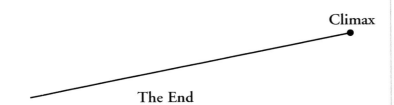

Climax

The End

There, that is all there is to creating your Plot Planner Form for The End of your story. The mini-breather you created, letting both your reader and your protagonist recover from

RELAX
BREATHE
TRUST THE PROCESS

The End portion of your project is roughly equal to The Beginning.

the Crisis to reflect on things, is over. Now it is time to start cranking up the tension and the conflicts again. Start plotting your scenes. The end is near. The stakes are high.

When you start to approach the final peak, stop and read on.

CLIMAX

Each scene in the steady trek builds in significance and relevance through rising tension and conflict until your protagonist reaches the true summit, the Climax of the entire story. This is where she is confronted by the biggest hurdle, greatest challenge, and toughest test. Will she react and revert back to her old, habitual ways, flaws and all? Or, will she act and step into her newly discovered power and show the world that she is a changed woman all the way to her core? Will she get what she wants? Now that she has what she thinks she wants, is she satisfied? What has she learned?

This final scene does not have to be an all-out war, full of explosions and death. What this final scene does have to have is meaning to the overall story.

When you know how the story is going to end, you then know every moment that must be dramatized to create a convincing and meaningful Climax. Work backward from the climax and dig for all the hows and whys in every action, every scene, and every detail to bring the story to that moment. Every word leads the reader to the inevitable but still surprising conclusion. All scenes must be thematically or structurally justified in the light of the Climax.

If a scene does not contribute to the climax, see if you can strengthen its cause and its effect. No? Then ask yourself if it can be cut without disturbing the impact of the ending? Yes?

Once you, as the writer, know how the character is going to play the final confrontation, you have all you need to know.

Arrange every scene and every detail as a sort of whisper to prepare the reader for the Climax. The reader may hope against hope how the story will end, but when the reader gets there, it should be obvious that there was absolutely no other possible ending.

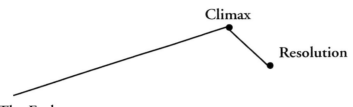

The Resolution is usually a brief tying up of most of the loose ends. There is no need to tie them all up. It is best not to have the resolution go on for too long. The energy of the story has dropped and, as much as the reader does not want the story to end, it is up to you, the writer, to end it. There is one magic moment to every experience. Prolong the resolution and your story becomes like the last guest to leave the party, a little woozy and worn-out.

PLOT THE THEMATIC SIGNIFICANCE

THE BEST FOR THE LAST

Months after readers have finished a great story, many cannot call up the action scenes or describe the actual character development. However, even years later, those same readers still hold an idea, if vague, of what the story was about. They remember the underlying theme.

FINDING YOUR THEME

Answer the following and you may find the theme of your story:

- What do you want the reader left with after she has finished reading your book?
- Why are you writing the book?
- What are you trying to say?

A great story weaves together three plotlines:
- **DRAMATIC ACTION,**
- **CHARACTER EMOTIONAL DEVELOPMENT,**
and
- **THEMATIC SIGNIFICANCE.**

• What is the overall conclusion you want your readers to walk away with?

Do not worry if you are unable to answer these questions until after you have written a draft or two. This is more common than not. Theme is best when it is not imposed on the story, but comes from within it. If you have not yet discovered the theme of your project, write the questions from above and tape it to your computer, then keep searching as you write.

Eventually, you do want to know the theme for two reasons:

1. Theme matters to the reader. Readers today are deluged with books and magazines and the Internet. For them to commit their precious time to reading your story, there has to be something in it for them beyond the pure enjoyment of reading your words. Theme defines what is at stake in your story.
2. The more clearly you can define your theme, the tighter your story. Once you know your theme, your scene choices will follow theme as opposed to other possibilities.

KNOW YOUR THEME

Once you know your theme, you can go back over your plotline and mark the scenes that show the theme. Trust the process; all the answers you need are in your story right now. It's up to you to find them. Your theme serves as a compass on your journey, determining what is on course in what you have

Your theme holds you to your subject.

written and where you have stumbled down a dead end or gone off the trail.

Once you know your theme, write it out in sentence form. This is what your book attempts to prove. Write it across the top of your Plot Planner, as a reminder to incorporate it into each and every scene through the use of details and choices and character emotional development.

SOMETHING TO PROVE

We usually write about something we care deeply about, or are interested in exploring, or are grappling with in our own lives, or simply find fascinating and want to learn more about.

Oftentimes, these themes originate from our own personal past. What images or experiences in your life have remained clear through the passage of time? The big traumatic moments pop right to the surface. Stay still and wait awhile. The next image to surface may surprise you. Buried in those experiences are beliefs by which you have lived your life.

THREE EXAMPLES:

1) One student remembered being chastised in front of her entire class in an early grade for challenging the teacher's words. Although she was ultimately proven right, the student never forgot the humiliation she suffered. With that one memory she discovered she had been living her life and writing her stories with the belief that speaking up and speaking out and speaking back comes at a price.

One way or another, you will prove something to your readers through your story.

2) An artist paints a picture of a garden. The colors and shading and composition of the piece are flawless and deserve attention. Another artist has a deep wound that has left her with the belief that people are no damn good. She paints the same garden, but integrates into the composition a pair of scissors.

3) A character's belief system directly influences the choices she makes. The following are three different reactions to the same experience based on three different belief systems. The protagonist is a single mother. She has children to feed. She is grateful to be hired on as a night watchman.

Once on the job, the woman hears screams and pleads come from the warehouse on the property. The boss is abusing the workers with a cattle prod. Workers beg for mercy as they are held against their will.

The boss instructs the woman to throw the switch to the electrical fence if any of the workers try to escape over the barbed wire. They will be electrocuted. The boss leaves.

Up until this point, the woman has shown disbelief on her face and discomfort in her body language, but, even so, she does as she is told. With the electric fence in play, the character must make a decision when the workers plead for mercy as they try to escape.

When the workers plead with her, if the protagonist believes that:

(1) to keep your job, you do what you are told, no matter how inhumane you believe it is, she will throw the switch.

When the workers plead with her,

(2) if protagonist believes that when someone is down, he should be kicked, she might not only throw switch, but she may also trip the workers as they attempt to escape.

(3) Or when the workers plead with her, if the theme of your story is that there comes a time in everyone's life when you have to take a stand, the protagonist refuses to throw the switch and quits the job.

In each segment, protagonist's theme in life plays directly into her particular story line.

EXPLANATION

No matter what we write, the process is an exploration into ourselves. Our own beliefs and themes pop up when we least expect it. Sometimes, we find what we thought were our beliefs do not translate onto the page, and so we must delve even deeper to find out what it is we truly believe.

If your characters show a mind of their own and deviate from the plot you envisioned for them, ask yourself if the resistance is coming from your inner self. Your deeper self may be begging for the opportunity to come into the light and force you to confront your real truth. Not the truth you were brought up to believe. Not the truth of the world around you. But your own authentic truth.

Themes are the fundamental and often universal ideas explored in fiction.

EXAMPLES OF THEME

- Things are not always what they appear. *To Kill a Mockingbird* by Harper Lee.
- Fascination with wealth is self-destructive. *The Great Gatsby* by F. Scott Fitzgerald.
- Beneath the surface of seemingly ordinary women lay extraordinary lives. *Stone Diaries* by Carol Shields.
- When a boy is coming of age and the only life he has ever known is disappearing into the past, in order to claim his place in the world, that boy must leave on a dangerous and harrowing journey. *All the Pretty Horses* by Cormac McCarthy.
- Through ambition and courage, man is able to survive against all odds. *The Sea-Wolf* by Jack London.
- To find a place for oneself, one must first break away. *White Oleander* by Janet Fitch.
- Home is where the heart is. *Where the Heart Is* by Billie Letts.
- There is a collective tendency of man to go overboard toward generosity and forgiveness. *The Adventures of Tom Sawyer* by Mark Twain.
- Man cannot escape his destiny but may be ennobled in the attempt. *Oedipus Rex* by Sophocles.
- Family loyalty leads to a life of crime. *The Godfather* by Mario Puzo.
- Forgiveness of others begins with forgiveness

of self. *Love Made of Heart* by Teresa LeYung Ryan.

• Courage leads to redemption. *The Old Man and the Sea* by Ernest Hemingway.

• Forced self-examination leads to generosity. *A Christmas Carol* by Charles Dickens.

• Even the most determined and ruthless psychiatric establishment cannot crush the human spirit. *One Flew Over the Cuckoo's Nest* by Ken Kesey.

• When left to their own devices, people naturally revert to cruelty, savagery, and barbarism. *Lord of the Flies* by William Golding.

• Affection, loyalty, and conscience are more important than social advancement, wealth, and class. *Great Expectations* by Charles Dickens.

• Independent ideas cannot always translate into a simultaneously self-sufficient and socially acceptable existence. *The Awakening* by Kate Chopin.

• Patterns of inequality in human rights based on racial differences are unjust and ultimately intolerable. *Cry, the Beloved Country* by Alan Paton.

• A person who learns the profound effect he/she has had on his/her family and community is given a renewed faith to live. *It's a Wonderful Life* story written by Philp Van Doren Stern, movie directed by Frank Capra.

• A tight-knit family, no matter how poor, can survive anything. *Grapes of Wrath* by John Steinbeck.

• Being different is a secret that all humans

share. *Stones from the River* by Ursula Hegi.
- Friends can fill an empty heart. *Because of Winn-Dixie* by Kate DiCamillo.
- The will to survive can bring material success yet paired with narcissism and a lack of compassion will lead to loss of love. *Gone with the Wind* by Margaret Mitchell.

In Closing

WHEN TO PLOT

I invite you to use the Scene Tracker and the Plot Planner in any way you find the most useful to your writing life. The following are three points in your writing you might find most valuable to use these forms.

1) PRE-PLOT

There seems to be two general categories of writers: those who do not pre-plot their writing projects before they begin, and those who do.

Writers who do not pre-plot are often referred to as intuitive writers. They prefer to work things out on the page. The other group of writers finds that making things up as they go with no advance planning is like flying without a net. Since the objective of this book is to support you in your writing, do what works for you.

I recommend that you plot out your writing project at least three times during a writing project:
- Pre-plot
- Revision
- Final Edit

A pre-plot is the place to put those ideas in some sort of order as you brainstorm, allowing the ideas to flow.

Each of us has some idea of what we want to say and why, long before we ever begin writing. Think of the pre-plot as a useful boundary that keeps out those things that might lead you astray in your writing or take you on a wild-goose chase down blind alleys.

The muse often feeds us images in the same way that dreams do: disjointed, symbolic, and metaphoric. A Plot Planner is a form in which the muse can pour the vision. Once you create a plot structure, then you are free to imagine anything you want within those confines. Or, as Wayne Muller writes in his book *Sabbath*, "... Imagine that certain limitations on our choices are actually seeds of great freedom."

Granted, this form, this pre-plot you create, will be a skeleton. You need not adhere too fervently to it. If you find you are pushing your characters around to fit into the grand design, and they dig in their heels, stop. Surrender, and see what happens next. Either way, before you undertake a project that could take months, possibly years, to complete, the more pre-planning and careful thought you give, the less time you will spend rewriting.

The first draft separates people who write from those who talk about writing.

2) REVISION

When you are ready to undertake a revision, it means you have arrived at a most important destination: completion of your first draft! Celebrate! The first draft is a test of faith and perseverance, and is a rite of passage of sorts.

Once the celebration is over, and before you start in on your first rewrite, (yes, there will be many more than one rewrite), reread your story to see what you have. Then, rather than just go back through your piece and move words around and call it a rewrite, I invite both the intuitive writers and the plotters both to take the time you need to carefully re-plot out your story. There is no better way to analyze your project than to do a complete re-plot based on what you have written. The process alone gives you a new vision or sense of the structure of your project so you know what to hone, refine, and focus on in the rewrite.

As you re-plot your story, look for openings where you can broaden and intensify the more subtle implications of your original insight. Look for ways to exploit your scenes by making them carry as much weight as they can bear. Make sure the scenes are working for the story on all levels—character, action, theme, and, where appropriate, historical and political significance. Does the reader always know the who, what, where, and when of the scene? Have you incorporated "showing" details? Is there tension and conflict? Do the characters experience some sort of emotional change in each and every scene? Are the scenes well written?

At this point, a unifying premise or central theme might reveal itself. Some of us require a few select trusted readers to uncover the thread. Whatever it takes to find it, that thread will be invaluable as you rewrite.

3) FINAL EDIT

At this point, exhaustion has likely stepped in, making it tempting to proclaim to all your patient and loyal family and friends that you are finally finished. Please do not shoot the messenger, but I would like to recommend that you first take a deep breath and do a final plotting of your story before you make the heady declaration.

Try re-plotting out your story before undertaking a rewrite.

Sign up for a **Plot Phone Consultation** from anywhere in the world. For more information, please visit: www.blockbusterplots.com

Plot out your story before you undertake the final edit to ensure that all the elements are in place.

For monthly Plot tips, sign-up for BLOCKBUSTER PLOTS eZine at www.BlockbusterPlots.com and click on Contact

THIS IS THE TIME TO TEST YOUR FINAL PRODUCT.

- Examine every detail, every word, every sentence, and every connection.
- Is every summary relevant to the action that follows?
- Does every detail contribute to the thematic significance and make the dramatic action and the character emotional development more believable?
- Is every action meaningful?
- Does every scene contribute to the whole?
- Is the conflict rising slowly as it should?
- Have you provided adequate suspense?
- Is your core conflict resolved?
- Have you seamlessly integrated your theme throughout the project?
- Is the story fulfilled?

Are you sure? Okay, then go for it. Shout it from the highest hill! You're finished! Congratulations!

APPENDICES

APPENDIX ONE:

PLOT PLANNER FORM

ABOVE THE LINE
SCENES THAT SHOW:

- Power is somewhere other than with the protagonist
- Tension
- Conflict
- Complications
- Loss of power by the protagonist
- Dramatic Action and movement
- Confrontations
- Turning points

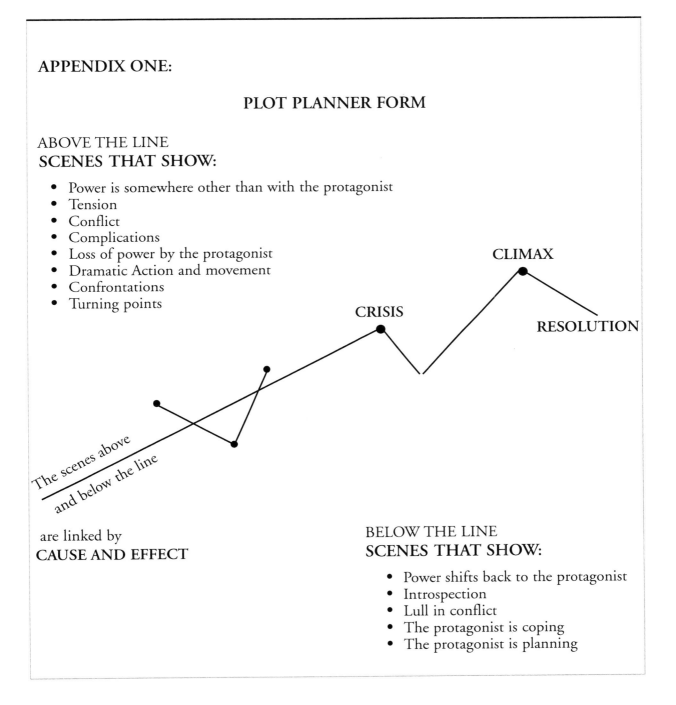

CLIMAX

CRISIS

RESOLUTION

The scenes above
and below the line

are linked by
CAUSE AND EFFECT

BELOW THE LINE
SCENES THAT SHOW:

- Power shifts back to the protagonist
- Introspection
- Lull in conflict
- The protagonist is coping
- The protagonist is planning

APPENDIX TWO:

SCENE TRACKER

First two chapters of *The Adventures of Tom Sawyer* by Mark Twain with the theme of: There is a collective tendency of man to go overboard toward generosity and forgiveness.

SCENE TRACKER — *The Adventures of Tom Sawyer* by Mark Twain

SC SU	DATES SETTING	CHARACTER EM. DEV.	GOAL	DRAMATIC ACTION	CONFLICT	CHANGE	THEME DETAIL
Chpt.1 SC #1	Fri. Aunt's House	T: Small, smart, fast, liar A:Softy Dead sis's son	Escape	Tom/Aunt Trouble	X	-/-/+	*T
SU							
SC#2	Fri. dinner		Not to be found out/cut school	Interrogated	X (Will he or won't he)	+/-/+/-	*T
SU				WHISTLING			
SC#3	Fri. Evening	Not one to fight right off	Figure out new boy	Fight Caught by A.	X (Will he or won't he)	+/-/-	Aunt forgave him earlier. Will he forgive new boy?
CHAPT.2							
SC#4	Sat. am Field	Hates work Intro: J;	To get out of work	Whitewash fence	X (Will he or won't he)	-/-	
SU				PAINTING			
SC#5	Minutes later	Clever	Get someone else to do work	Ignores friend Friend falls for it	X (Will he or won't he)	+/+	T. ends up with friends paying him to work

APPENDIX THREE:

PLOT PLANNER

First two chapters of *The Adventures of Tom Sawyer* by Mark Twain

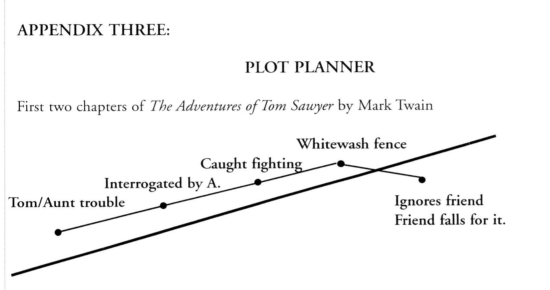

ANALYSIS

Above the Line and Below the Line:
Scene One and Scene Two (Chapter One) belong above the line because Tom, the protagonist, is not in control; his aunt is, at least she is until he escapes.
Scene Three also belongs above the line because a fight ensues and then Tom is caught by his Aunt who has had just about enough of his antics.
Scene Four (Chapter Two) belongs above the line because of Tom is not in charge. His scene goal, which is to get out of having to do his work, sets up the tension of "will he succeed or won't he?" This same sort of tension continues in Scene Five (Chapter Two) in that we know Tom is clever, but no one is clever enough to convince a friend to do his work for him, or is he? The scene ends below the line because Tom is that clever. Not only is he clever enough to get his friends to do his work, they actually pay him to do it.

Cause and Effect:
Scene One and Scene Two are linked because Aunt is looking for Tom in Scene One. Because of that, in Scene Two she finds him. Because she finds him, he escapes. Because he escapes he spots the new boy in town. Because of that, Tom gets in a fight. Because he fights and gets caught he gets punished. And so on...

APPENDIX FOUR:

CHARACTER EMOTIONAL/PSYCHOLOGICAL PLOT INFORMATION

A Lesson Before Dying by Ernest J. Gaines.
THEME: It is heroic to resist and defy the expected.

Protagonist's name: Grant Wiggins

Overall story goal: For Grant to impart his learning and his pride to Jefferson, a young black man who has been wrongly convicted of murder and sentenced to death.

Protagonist's personal goal: To escape the quarter and marry Vivian

Protagonist's dream: To prove to whites that blacks are equal.

What stands in his way? Grant's fear and secret, and Jefferson's resistance.

What does he/she stand to lose, if not successful (risk)? The respect of his aunt, Jefferson's godmother, his community and the woman he loves.

Flaw or greatest fault? His inclination to run away from conflict and unpleasantness or anything he just might fail at accomplishing.

Greatest strength? His intelligence and compassion

Hates? Plantation school, teaching, running in place

Loves? Vivian

Fears? That he will fail.

Secret? That his mentor is right—that those who do not run away will die a violet death or be brought down to the level of beasts.

APPENDIX FIVE:

PLOT PLANNER

A Lesson Before Dying by Ernest J. Gaines.
THEME: It is heroic to resist and defy the expected.

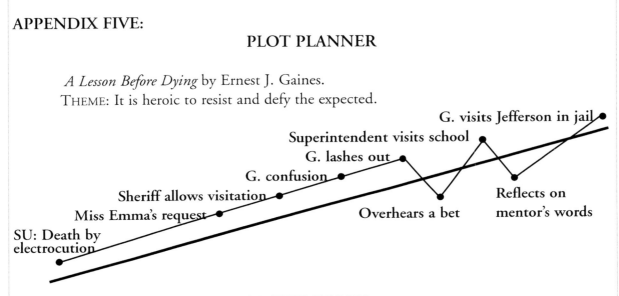

THE BEGINNING PORTION OF THE STORY

The story begins in Summary, establishing the overarching conflict: an innocent man is sentenced to death by electrocution. This causes Miss Emma's request, which in turns causes Grant's desperate wish to "get away from here."

When the sheriff agrees to allow Grant visitation rights with the prisoner, the stakes grow ever higher. Grant does not say yes, but he does not say no, either. Vivian asks him to "go for us."

Because of the pressure that is on Grant, he lashes out at his students, which in turn causes him feel that what he does is worthless.

Grant overhears a bet. This causes him to ask himself, am I to act like a teacher or like "the n_____ I am expected to be?" He takes back control and decides to help Jefferson die with dignity.

In the next scene, the white superintendent visits the school. Although the superintendent humiliates him, Grant waves goodbye as he is expected to.

In the next scene, Grant reflects on Jefferson who sat in the same classroom just a few years back. That causes Grant to remember his mentor's words.

In the final scene of The Beginning portion of the book, Grant visits Jefferson in jail.

The Beginning portion of *A Lesson before Dying*, introduces the characters, establishes most of the protagonist's Character Emotional/Psychological Plot Information, introduces the theme, begins with an enormous dilemma and ends on a cliff-hanger. The Beginning portion ends almost exactly on the page 1/4 of the total page count of the novel.

APPENDIX SIX:

Grapes of Wrath
by John Steinbeck

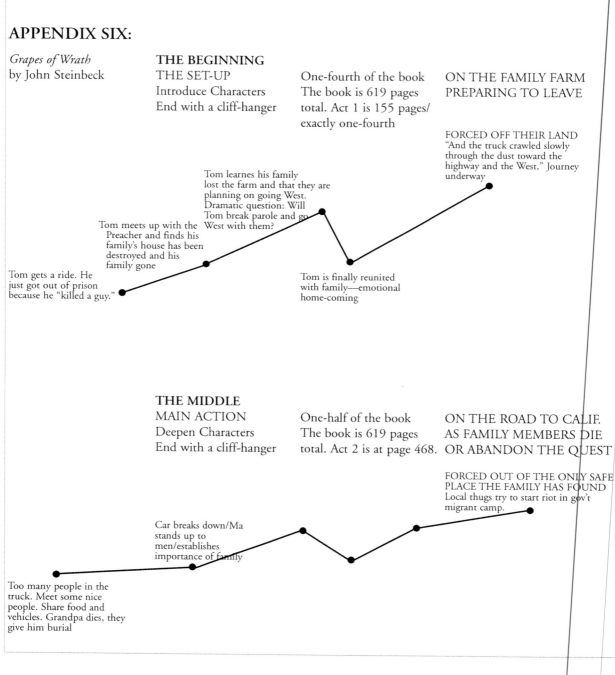

THE BEGINNING
THE SET-UP
Introduce Characters
End with a cliff-hanger

One-fourth of the book
The book is 619 pages
total. Act 1 is 155 pages/
exactly one-fourth

ON THE FAMILY FARM
PREPARING TO LEAVE

FORCED OFF THEIR LAND
"And the truck crawled slowly
through the dust toward the
highway and the West," Journey
underway

Tom learnes his family
lost the farm and that they are
planning on going West.
Dramatic question: Will
Tom break parole and go
West with them?

Tom meets up with the
Preacher and finds his
family's house has been
destroyed and his
family gone

Tom gets a ride. He
just got out of prison
because he "killed a guy."

Tom is finally reunited
with family—emotional
home-coming

THE MIDDLE
MAIN ACTION
Deepen Characters
End with a cliff-hanger

One-half of the book
The book is 619 pages
total. Act 2 is at page 468.

ON THE ROAD TO CALIF.
AS FAMILY MEMBERS DIE
OR ABANDON THE QUEST

FORCED OUT OF THE ONLY SAFE
PLACE THE FAMILY HAS FOUND
Local thugs try to start riot in gov't
migrant camp.

Car breaks down/Ma
stands up to
men/establishes
importance of family

Too many people in the
truck. Meet some nice
people. Share food and
vehicles. Grandpa dies, they
give him burial

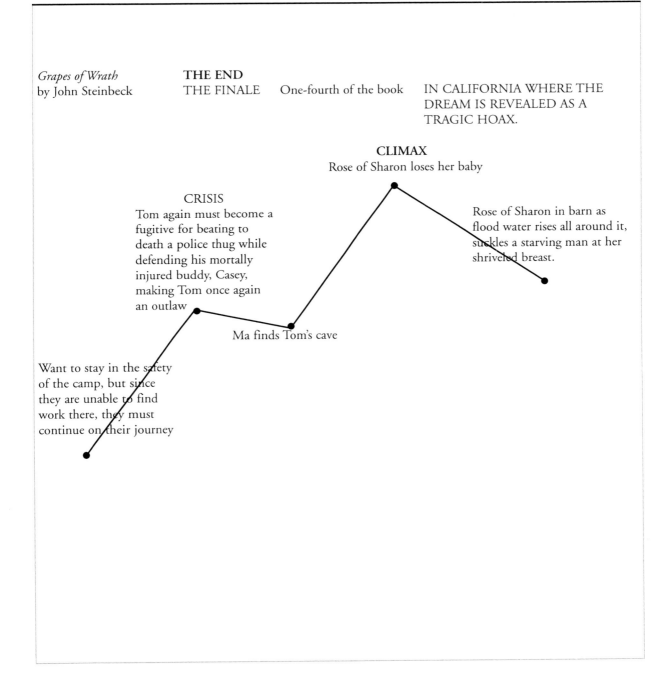

Grapes of Wrath
by John Steinbeck

THE END
THE FINALE

One-fourth of the book

IN CALIFORNIA WHERE THE
DREAM IS REVEALED AS A
TRAGIC HOAX.

CLIMAX
Rose of Sharon loses her baby

CRISIS

Tom again must become a
fugitive for beating to
death a police thug while
defending his mortally
injured buddy, Casey,
making Tom once again
an outlaw

Rose of Sharon in barn as
flood water rises all around it,
suckles a starving man at her
shriveled breast.

Ma finds Tom's cave

Want to stay in the safety
of the camp, but since
they are unable to find
work there, they must
continue on their journey

INDEX

Products and Services
Available from ILLUSION PRESS

Please feel free to email contact@blockbusterplots.com for more information on any of these products and services.

SERVICES

Plot Consultation
Plot Consultation takes place over the telephone from anywhere in the world. Each writer receives a Plot Planner for their individual project based on their scenes.

BLOCKBUSTER PLOTS eZine
This is a free monthly service full of plot tips, inspiration, contests and events. Sign-up today. Email: contact@blockbusterplots.com

PRODUCTS

Book: *BLOCKBUSTER PLOTS Pure & Simple* (ISBN 1-877809-19-5) shows writers strategies that demystify the structure of story on a scene and plot level both.

Kit: Scene Tracker Kit to dramatically cut the time it takes to finish your story. Includes: Blockbuster Plots book, Scene Tracker DVD, Scene Tracker CD.

Writers Workshops DVDs:
1) 7 Essential Elements of Scene, using F. Scott Fitzgerald's *The Great Gatsby*
2) The Ultimate Guide to Creating Plot, using Arthur Golden's *Memoirs of a Geisha*
3) Seven Secrets of Plot, using John Steinbeck's *Grapes of Wrath*
4) Plot Guide for Children's Book Authors, using Gennifer Choldenko's *Al Capone Does My Shirts*

CD:
The Scene Tracker Template CD is a visual tool that allows writers to actually "see" whether or not each individual scene in their projects advances the action plot of the story, develops the character, contributes to the theme, provides tension, conflict and suspence, and reflects a change in attitude or circumstances.

For more information, please visit: www.blockbusterplots.com